Woodturning in Miniature

Woodturning
in Miniature

Ian and Nina Wilkie

The Crowood Press

First published in 2001 by
The Crowood Press Ltd
Ramsbury, Marlborough
Wiltshire SN8 2HR

British Library Cataloguing-in-Publication Data
A catalogue record for this book is available from the British Library.

ISBN 1 86126 471 2

Photographs by Nina Wilkie

Line drawings by Keith Field

Photograph previous page: Small bud vases and bowls turned in yew and laburnum.

Typeset by Textype Typesetters, Cambridge

Printed and bound in Malaysia by Times Offset (M) Sdn. Bhd.

CONTENTS

A hollow form bottle (described in Exercise 10) in cherry and rosewood. On the left a small bowl in elm and on the right an elm bowl with a folded-over top.

A burr-elm bowl on the left and a quaiche on the right.

INTRODUCTION

It has been my intention to write this book for a number of years, in an effort to bring together, under one cover, the techniques and equipment I use when turning miniatures in wood and alternative materials. I have written many magazine articles on the subject and tested many lathes, chucks, turning tools, drives and centres, and I would like to share the knowledge I have acquired with other enthusiasts who, I hope, will gain as much pleasure as I do from this fascinating form of turning.

How small is miniature and how minute is micro? Some items turned are the correct size and just happen to be small: knobs for a cabinet, nutcrackers, lace bobbins, pens or pieces of jewellery, for instance. Other examples are miniaturized versions of the real things: furniture and fittings for a doll's house, cannons and dead-eyes for a model ship or small turned parts for other modelling hobbies come to mind.

Miniature woodturning is a more precise practice than general wood-turning and very much akin to model engineering in wood, where accuracy and measurement are all-important. Working in a smaller scale has many advantages. The woodturner has the opportunity to use interesting, exotic wood because small blanks are more affordable. Moreover, if a miniature lathe is being used the space required in the workshop is very much reduced; indeed, this form of wood-turning can be carried out without a workshop if one is not available, and most of the equipment can be put away if necessary. Using a conventional lathe can be noisy: if the woodturner lives in a flat, or in close proximity to others, this can be

Native woods from the garden: plum on the left, yew in the centre and laburnum on the right.

a problem. If, however, a miniature lathe is used, which is so much quieter, the neighbours are not likely to be antagonized; indeed, they are more likely to be fascinated! Another advantage is that these lathes can be operated from a sitting position if standing for long periods is a problem.

There is no reason why small-scale and micro turning cannot be carried out on a full-sized lathe with the right equipment, and I have made suggestions for this, but this book is primarily written to illustrate what can be achieved on a much smaller lathe. I know many people, myself included, who are fortunate to have both a large lathe and a miniature lathe, so they have the best of both worlds.

When I first started woodturning I had a growing family and spent what little I could afford on my hobby with great planning and deliberation, relying on Christmas and birthday presents for additional equipment, and I scoured the woodworking shows for bargains! I am keenly aware that most people have a budget for their hobby but today, with the explosion of interest in woodturning, the large number of woodworking shows and all the attractive advertising, it can be confusing and difficult to select the right equipment for the sort of turning the woodturner wishes to carry out, and the wrong choice can be expensive. In this book I have only featured equipment which I have used for a long period and know to be reliable and of good quality; some items will be very specialized and only of interest to a few turners, but they do illustrate the wide range of work that can be undertaken. It is far better to add accessories slowly as the need arises, rather than to race out and buy on impulse. The aim should be to gradually build up a collection of good quality equipment which will last for many years and will suit the particular type of turning the woodturner wants to do. I have started with the lathe, the basic tools and simple accessories to show that with planning and ingenuity there is very little that cannot be turned. In time, when budgets allow, and as your confidence and skill increases, a chuck and further accessories can always be added. Woodturning in miniature is fascinating and it is fun to do, so I hope you will be inspired to ‘have a go’.

Ian Wilkie

— 1 —

THE WORKSHOP

Woodturning on a small scale is ideal for woodworkers who do not have much room for their hobby. One of my lectures, entitled 'Turning on the Kitchen Table', may raise eyebrows, but it can be done! At the other end of the scale, the lucky few may have a purpose-built, double-glazed and heated workshop or a dedicated room in the house, along with a shed to store timber. In between, workshops are set up in all sorts of spaces – at one end of a garage, in a garden shed (often shared with a lawnmower) or even (in my case, at one time) in a old coal shed! Benches can be constructed from old tables and kitchen units, and tools kept in cigar boxes or hand-built, customized wooden cases.

With careful planning, and selection of the most appropriate equipment, woodturning can be carried out in the smallest of areas, and high standards can be achieved. However, if you do decide to build a workshop or buy a shed, go for the biggest you can afford, because you will inevitably acquire more equipment and timber than you expected.

SETTING UP A WORKSHOP

When setting up a workshop, you need to give careful consideration to a number of the following factors.

LIGHTING

Good lighting is essential when producing small-scale work. Daylight is best and a

Large windows provide natural light in the author's workshop. When turning very small work, a ring lamp with a magnifying lens in the centre can be pulled down over the lathe (this is the Tyme Little Gem), to inspect the piece more closely. The lamp fits in a floor stand, so there is no possibility of vibration. The grey anti-slip matting and the rubber feet on the baseboard stop the lathe moving about on the bench.

large, opening window is very desirable. An angle-poise lamp, fitted with a 11w economy lamp producing light equivalent to a normal 60w bulb, is useful. These lamps are cool, long-lasting and economical. The lamp should be positioned close to the lathe, so that it can be pulled nearer to the work for critical inspection.

For very tiny work, consider using a daylight ring lamp, which incorporates a 1.75 magnifying lens. This amount of magnification, perhaps combined with ordinary reading glasses, is more than adequate. A × 10-hand magnifier is also very useful for assessing the quality of the work in daylight and for examining the cutting edges on tools.

Painting the workshop walls white, particularly around the lathe, can help to reflect light.

Generally, fluorescent lighting is not recommended in a workshop because it can cause a stroboscopic effect. This means that at certain speeds, work appears to be stationery when it is in fact rotating.

ELECTRICITY

A professional electrician should be consulted when fitting out a workshop for the use of power tools and machines. An adequate supply of power points is essential. It makes sense to have a central residual circuit device (RCD), particularly if the workshop is outside in a shed or garage. A tangle of wires, extension leads and multiple adapters is asking for trouble.

Check all plugs, leads and sockets at least once a year for signs of wear. Wood dust tends to build up inside plugs and wires can quickly work loose.

HEATING

Heating in the workshop is important for comfortable working all year round. A warm environment is much more inviting than a cold, damp garage and warm hands are more flexible and less likely to be damaged. The ideal is a heater that produces a low, constant heat, controlled by a thermostat and a time mechanism. This will not only make the space more pleasant to work in, but will also reduce the risk of condensation on tools and machinery which is more likely to occur if the workshop is heated for only short periods at a time.

Electric tube heaters, intended specifically for workshops, garages and greenhouses, are the most economical to run; oil-filled radiators are also suitable, but running costs are higher. Those with an internal workshop may be able to add an extra radiator or storage heater to their main central heating system. Garages and sheds can be double lined and insulated to protect against the risk of condensation; this will also help reduce the effects of noise emitted from machines.

Heaters with an open element are dangerous because fine dust and shavings are combustible. Fan heaters blow the dust around and soon become clogged up. Gas and paraffin heaters generate condensation and a live flame in a dusty atmosphere is not to be recommended.

FLOORING

The floor needs to be level, comfortable to stand on for long periods and easy to clean. One option is a floor made of concrete, skimmed over to make it uniform and with vinyl laid on top. The vinyl makes sweeping up and vacuuming easy. It may be advisable to cover a wooden floor with a sheet of chipboard or MDF so that it is firm and level for a machine. This will have the added benefit of making the floor draughtproof.

STORAGE

The main enemies to guard against are damp, dust, damage and loss. Chucks, drives and centres, together with all their small accessories, will quickly deteriorate and parts will be lost if they are not stored efficiently. A tidy and well-organized workshop is a pleasure to work in. Hanging tools on the workshop walls may look quaint and traditional, but they soon

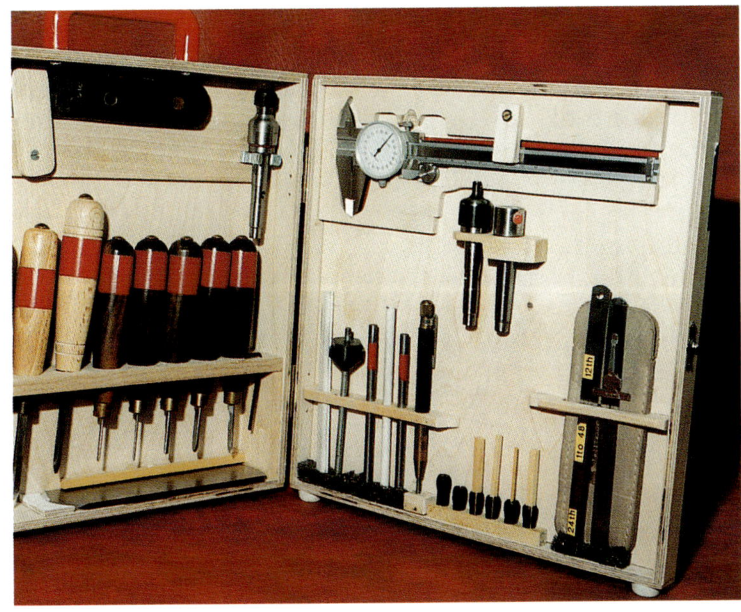

This fitted-out plywood box houses the equipment used by the author to demonstrate miniature woodturning at shows and clubs.

A small metal filing cabinet with ten shallow drawers stores all the miniature woodturning equipment used in this book. The drawer pulled out at the top holds the Marlin system. The drawer further down is customized to take all the measuring instruments and the other drawers are similarly fitted out. The cabinet is on castors and is easily moved around the workshop.

become covered in dust.

Throwing chisels and gouges into tool boxes, although preferable to hanging them up on racks, is disorganized and risky.

One option is to make a simple plywood hinged box (*see* the picture on page 11) to take turning tools, measuring equipment, drives and centres. A box like this can stand open on a bench or can be hung on a wall and then closed after work has finished for the day. Each tool has its place; any missing items can be spotted at a glance; and the cutting edges of the chisels and gouges are protected. One of the advantages of miniature turning is that the equipment need not take up too much room!

For a larger storage unit, consider a metal office filing cabinet (*see* the picture on page 11); mine is 610mm high × 280mm wide × 410mm deep and has ten shallow drawers. Castors on the base enable the unit to be moved easily around the workshop and stored away under the bench. Each drawer is customized to take the tools and the bases are lined with non-slip matting so that tools stay in place. In this way, the equipment is kept together, easily located and well protected against loss, damage, rust and dust.

Quite heavy machines can be kept on the adjustable shelves of taller, lockable metal office cupboards. The miniature lathe can be stored in a cupboard when not in use, together with other tools and machines.

WORKING SURFACES

All the working surfaces in the workshop should be at the same level and at a height that is comfortable for the woodturner. The woodworking bench should have two fitted vices; place blocks under the legs if you need to raise the height of the bench. A vinyl-covered working surface with cupboards underneath is also useful.

The area will remain totally flexible if no machines are fitted to the surfaces or

The six Ashley Iles miniature turning tools used throughout the book in a drawer in the cabinet.

worktops. For instructions on building a dedicated stand for a miniature lathe, which can be dismantled, *see* Chapter 2.

DUST

Woodturning, even in miniature, creates copious amounts of shavings, together with lots of fine wood dust produced during the sanding stages. Sometimes you seem to end up with more wood than you started with! In miniature turning, you tend to lean very close to the work, too, so it is wise to wear a disposable mask. Keep it on until the dust and shavings have been cleared up and vacuumed away at the end of a turning session. The mask should be clearly stamped with the letters and European standard numbers EN149FFP2S. Unmarked masks may be cheaper, but

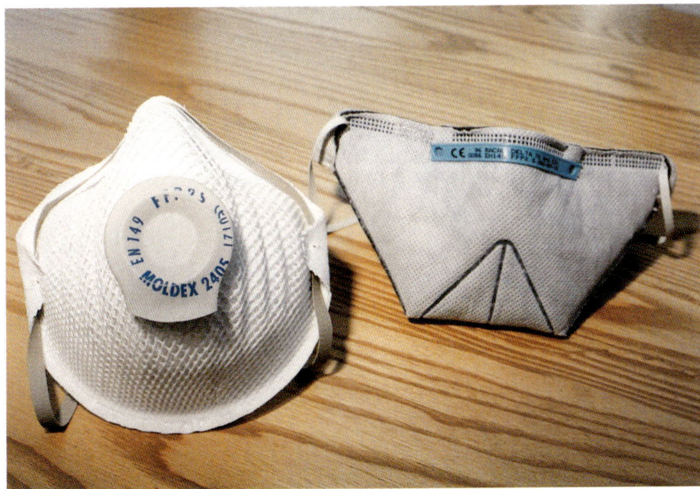

Two types of disposable mask that conform with the European Standard. The Moldex mask (left) has a hard shell and a valve that makes it particularly good for spectacle wearers; the Racal Delta mask (right) is a softer design, which folds flat neatly.

The Trend Airshield Respirator with rechargeable batteries offers full face protection and effective filtering of fine dust.

they will not filter out the fine, harmful dust particles. If you wear glasses, look for a mask fitted with a valve in the front to direct exhaled air downwards. This reduces the likelihood of the glasses being fogged up.

Respirators powered by rechargeable batteries also offer full face protection, and are cool and comfortable to wear, but they are expensive and need to be kept charged up. If you have an existing respiratory problem, seek advice from your doctor on the level of protection that you need.

Dust from some timbers can also cause irritation and rashes to exposed skin. This may be prevented by wearing a turning smock with tight cuffs and a close-fitting neck, showering quickly after a turning session, using a barrier cream on hands and face, or avoiding particular woods all together.

There are many dust extraction systems on sale at woodworking shows and in suppliers' catalogues. Although extraction is undoubtedly very helpful these are expensive, large and noisy machines. If you only do a little miniature woodturning occasionally, a vacuum round when you have finished is probably quite sufficient. If you do have an extractor, hold the pipe as near to the rotating wood as possible when you are sanding, to collect a proportion of the dust.

> A warm and comfortable workshop will always be a pleasure to work in.

— 2 —

THE WOODTURNING LATHE

Miniatures may be turned on a woodturning lathe of standard size (*see* page 19), but it is also possible to buy a miniature lathe (*see below*) that has been designed specifically for this type of woodturning. Modellers will be familiar with the Unimat; if only the smallest of miniatures are to be turned, the Unimat Woodturning Variant should be considered (*see* page 21).

MINIATURE LATHES

Note: the 12-volt drill-powered miniature lathe is not suitable for the serious woodturner. It lacks power, does not accept morse taper fittings and its overall rigidity is poor; these lathes are not featured in this book.

There are many full-sized woodturning lathes on the market, but the range of miniature lathes is limited to around half a dozen machines. In all cases, the design criteria are very similar, however. A miniature lathe should be a scaled-down version of its bigger brother, and not inferior in any way.

FEATURES

When selecting a lathe for miniature work, the following points should be carefully considered:

- *Accuracy*: the headstock and tailstock must line up when viewed from above (vertically) and from the side (horizontally). The main spindle should rotate accurately without any play.
- *Rigidity*: a lathe needs to be rigid in construction, with a strong headstock, bed, tailstock and toolrest assembly. No part of the lathe should vibrate or resonate when the machine is in operation.
- *Headstock*: the spindle should be threaded so that screw-on accessories can be attached. It is an advantage if the

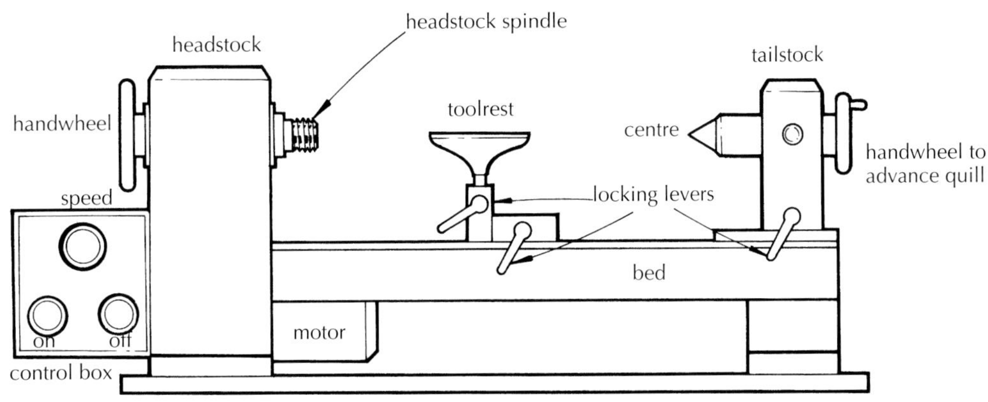

Parts of a miniature woodturning lathe.

spindle is drilled to take standard 1MT fittings and if it is hollow throughout so that these can be easily ejected.

- *Tailstock*: the tailstock must move smoothly over the bed and be capable of being locked firmly in position. Fine adjustment should be possible by means of a handwheel, which rotates to advance or retract the quill. A quill travel of at least 50mm is recommended.

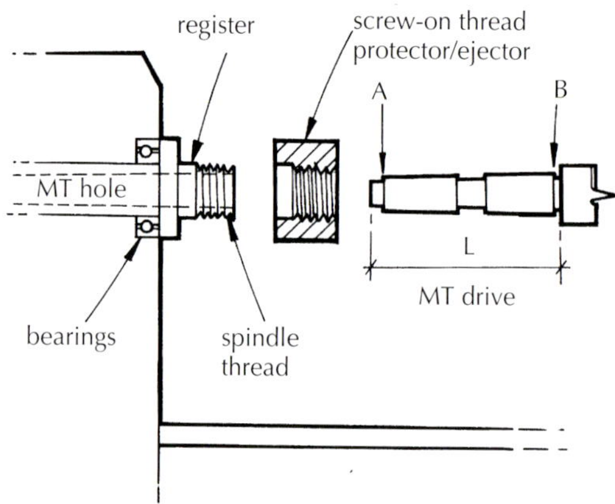

Cross section of the headstock.

The Selbix Mini headstock has built-in indexing and a key is used to select the settings. The second key on the ring locks the headstock in position. The nut on the outboard end of the hollow spindle is holding a draw-bar for the Marlin drive carrier.

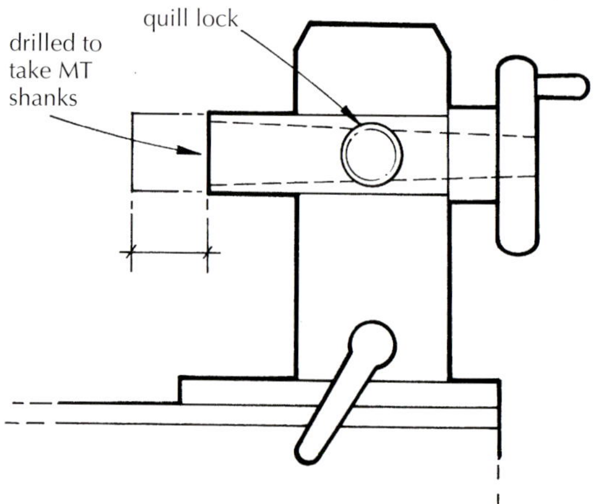

Parts of the tailstock.

The Selbix Mini tailstock has cam-action locking on both the tailstock and the toolrest assembly.

- *Distances and diameters*: with a revolving centre fitted and a drive there should be at least 150mm between centres and at least 50mm available over the bed bars for faceplate turning.
- *Toolrest*: the link between the tool and the wood to be turned: the toolrest should be both rigid and well finished. It must be in line with the centre line of the lathe when viewed horizontally and capable of being adjusted close to the

The tailstock on the Selbix Mini lathe can be slid back and simply lifted out, giving more access to work on the headstock if tailstock support is not needed.

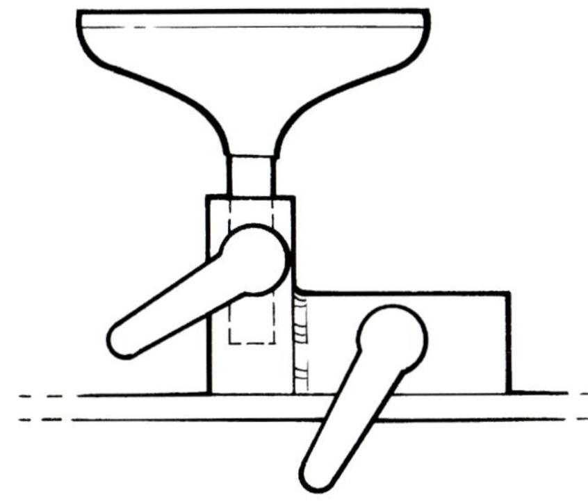

The toolrest assembly.

work, moreover it is important that it can be raised above the centre line and lowered well below the centre line as required. Two sizes will be needed: a standard 100mm and a shorter 50mm toolrest.

- *Levers*: the locking devices on the toolrest and tailstock assemblies should work effectively, be easy to use and not get in the way when turning is in progress or clash with each other.
- *Motor*: the motor should be as quiet as possible so that any noise emitted is not a nuisance to others or a problem for the turner when working. It should be attached permanently to the machine because it makes a neater unit. Switches and controls should be well positioned and positive for reasons of safety.
- *Speed*: a really high speed is needed in miniature work and the lathe should give up to 4,000rpm. Most miniature lathes have electronic speed control. One even has a control box separate from the machine, which offers a couple of advantages: first, the controls can be positioned exactly where the turner wants them, and second, the box, which is heavy, can be detached from the lathe. This may be relevant if the lathe has to be lifted up and stored away. The electronics must deliver sufficient power throughout the whole speed range.
- *Design*: the lathe should be neat, compact and not too heavy. Again, this may be particularly important if you have no workshop and need to put the lathe away in a box or a cupboard after use.

The APTC Carbatec MkII miniature lathe has a separate box that plugs into the lathe and houses the sophisticated, solid-state, electronic speed controls and the on/off switch. It also has cam-action locking on both the tailstock and toolrest assembly.

The Tyme Little Gem miniature lathe is small enough to be stored, with its baseboard, in a large plastic tool box when not in use. It is a pleasure to use, but is not in production at the moment.

The Rexon miniature lathe gives 460mm between centres. This is a relatively inexpensive lathe with built-in electronic variable speed.

- *Finish*: in miniature work the turner's fingers are very close to the rotating work, so all parts of the machine need to be smooth without any sharp edges that could cause injury to fingers.

Although they are not essential, the following features would also be desirable:

- built-in indexing in the headstock offering twenty-four divisions;
- a handwheel on the outboard end of the headstock spindle, allowing it to be rotated by hand. This is useful when carefully checking work before removing it, and makes indexing easier;
- 300mm distance between centres and an increased diameter of 100mm available over the bed bars, to allow a greater range of turning;
- an industrially rated motor, which can be used for long periods without rest.

It is not an advantage to have a swivelling headstock on a small lathe. Turning blanks that are too big for the lathe could result in damage to the lathe bearings.

SETTING UP

Miniature lathes do not come with a stand. The decision on how to mount the machine will depend on whether the lathe and its stand will be left out, or whether it will have to be stored away after use. In either case, the lathe must be positioned at the correct working height for the individual turner, and the stand or bench must be rigid. If the lathe is too low, the operator will soon experience a stiff neck and sore shoulder muscles; if the stand wobbles or vibrates, the work will be poor.

An old kitchen unit or chest of drawers will probably not be good enough, and a simple, dedicated stand is usually the best option. The stand pictured below is inexpensive to make and can be dismantled and stored away if required. The lathe simply straddles the top. The strong saw-horse fittings are made of heavy-duty plastic and it is simple to cut the legs to achieve the correct height for the turner.

When working, keep the top surface of the stand completely clear of tools and accessories. They have a habit of bouncing around and falling off, and small accessories lost in the shavings will be in danger of being vacuumed up!

The advantages of a simple stand like this are that it will be inexpensive to make; it can be custom-built to suit the individual turner's height; there is plenty of leg room underneath; it is suitable for turners who choose to operate from a sitting position; and it is easy to sweep up shavings around the legs without obstruction.

The disadvantages of a storage unit with the lathe on top are that the arrangement is unnecessarily bulky; items stored in the drawers often vibrate and resonate during turning; shavings and dust get into the drawers; and there is restricted leg space, which can be a problem for the turner who wishes to sit at the lathe. Although it may seem a good idea to put the unit on wheels, lockable castors of a sufficiently high quality are very expensive.

USING A FULL-SIZED LATHE

Miniatures can be turned using a full-sized lathe but, in order to work safely and

Constructing a custom-built stand with saw-horse brackets for a miniature lathe. The legs can be released and the stand stored away when not in use.

accurately, it will be necessary to invest in some additional equipment. To produce good, detailed, accurate work the turner needs first to have confidence in that equipment, and then to use skill and imagination, and the right technique.

TOOLREST

The right toolrest is vital. In miniature woodturning it is important to get really close to the work and the turner needs to be able to get a finger under the toolrest, in order to support very small items. The toolrest needs to be rigid and firm. Standard toolrests are usually too bulky, but may be modified using a hacksaw and file, to make them more suitable for small-scale work.

REVOLVING CENTRE

A good quality revolving centre with a small diameter body for the tailstock will be needed.

DRILL CHUCK

The turner may well already have a good-quality Jacob's-type drill chuck to fit in the tailstock. If it proves to be too bulky, other possibilities are described in Chapter 3.

COMBINATION CHUCK

The turner who has a standard-sized lathe will usually already own a chuck and a selection of jaws. Many combination chucks, even if they are efficient and well made, are unsuitable for small-scale work because they are too bulky. In most cases, the sharp edges of the jaws pose a threat when the turner is working close to the headstock. For information on small chucks that are suitable for use on a full-sized lathe, *see* Chapter 3.

SPEED

The normal rule is, 'the smaller the diameter, the faster the lathe speed'. Turning a spindle of 1mm diameter requires the very highest speed the lathe will give. Most of the miniature lathes have a top speed of 5,000rpm, while a full-sized lathe rarely exceeds 3,000rpm and is more likely to have a maximum speed of around 2,000rpm. This can be a disadvantage but, with good technique, suitable wood and really sharp tools, together with accurate chucking, good results may still be achieved.

THE UNIMAT

My first miniature lathe was a Unimat 1 metal-turning lathe, which I used for woodturning in conjunction with a variety of improvised drives and faceplates and a small home-made toolrest. About ten years ago I replaced it with a Unimat PC.

The more recent Emco Unimat 4 wood lathe variant is truly a miniature lathe. It is mounted on a polished plywood base, which has a drawer that is useful for storing tools and accessories. The machine is supplied with a cup chuck and a small prong drive, but the latter is disappointing and worth replacing. Because the Unimat is so small, and weighs less than 6kg, it is easily stored in a plastic toolbox or a custom-built wooden box. If it is used off its base, it will tip over. The cast-iron bed is accurately machined and there are quality bearings in the headstock, which is bored throughout 10.2mm.

The model in the picture on page 21 is belt driven over a series of pulleys to give eight speeds. Speed changing is easy, with the drive pulleys fully guarded by a

The Unimat Woodturning Variant miniature lathe is very small!

strong plastic guard. A more expensive, variable-speed model is also available. The on/off NVR switch is mounted above the motor, just behind the headstock. Operating a two-speed switch behind the on/off switch means that at the fastest settings, in the slow position, the speed is 240rpm and, at the fast position, the speed is 4,000rpm, with similar ratios with other belt settings. The tailstock is machined in cast alloy with a calibrated handwheel. The headstock and tailstock have the same spindle thread size of 14 × 1mm.

The main stumbling block with this lathe is that the headstock and tailstock are not drilled to take 1MT standard accessories. The lathe is a conversion from a very effective metalworking lathe, of watch-making standard, so it is not possible to re-bore the headstock and tailstock spindles to take 1MT fittings – there just is not enough metal. The best solution is to fit a Multistar Micro chuck (*see* Chapter 3, page 27), together with a 1MT tool carrier, so that standard accessories can be used. Although Unimat's own three-jaw self-centring chuck is ideal for metalwork, it is not recommended for woodturning because the jaws could be hazardous to the turner.

Unimat offers some good-quality, but expensive accessories for this lathe, including a faceplate, a screw-on 6mm

The Unimat Woodturning Variant miniature lathe comes mounted on a plywood box with a drawer, which will take all the bits and pieces needed for very small-scale work. The lathe is shown fitted with a Multistar Micro chuck and its carrier, holding a 6mm Marlin collet chuck in the headstock and the Unimat revolving centre screwed on to the tailstock.

capacity drill chuck and a screw-on revolving centre.

This is a very small lathe, with a maximum distance between centres of 200mm and a maximum diameter of 92mm. This means that it is only suitable for truly miniature turning. With the chuck fitted with a drive in the headstock, and with a revolving centre in the tailstock, the distance between centres is reduced to 100mm. This distance may seem very limited, but it should be enough for miniature-scale work. For example, in 1/12th scale, 200mm represents 48in, and it is unlikely that the turner would want to produce items any larger than this.

Scale modellers, who only want to turn very small items, should consider this machine seriously. Adding a cross-slide, tool holder, leadscrew and three-jaw self-centring chuck turns it into a miniature metal-turning lathe as well. With the saw table, this very versatile precision machine is always a delight to use.

CARE AND MAINTENANCE OF LATHES

Any woodturning lathe requires regular cleaning and maintenance if it is to be kept in good condition:

- Clean away any wood dust and shavings from the surfaces at the end of a session. Sawdust attracts moisture, which will lead to rust in all the nooks and crannies found in the smallest lathes.
- Use a thread protector whenever possible. This will protect the headstock spindle and make it easy to eject MT fittings without needing to hammer them out.
- Keep the headstock spindle thread clean and lightly oil the thread using a cloth and 3-in-1 oil. Do not use a spray oil such as WD40 because there is a risk that the oil will penetrate and dissolve the lubrication inserted by the manufacturer to protect the lathe bearings.
- Clean the MT hole in the headstock

The circular saw attachment fits over the bed of the Unimat lathe and only takes minutes to set up. The fine-toothed, hollow-ground blade will give a mirror finish on the wood being cut; the coarser blade (on the table) is used for rough cutting.

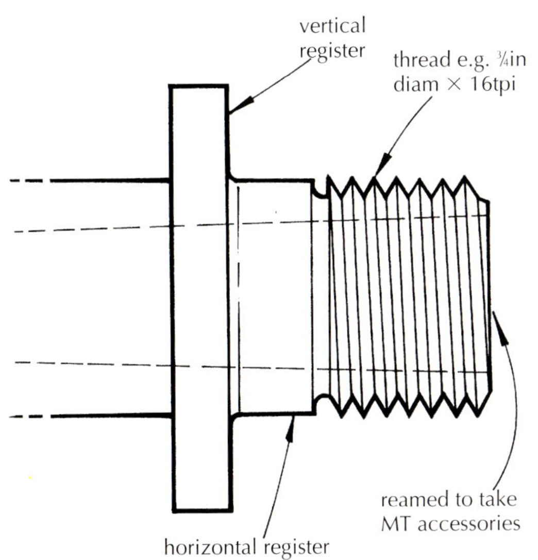

The headstock spindle thread.

and the tailstock using a cloth and 3-in-1 oil, or a proprietary tool sold for the purpose.

- Keep the toolrest edge smooth and free of nicks.
- Check electric cables regularly for any signs of wear.
- Lightly oil the bed bars and tailstock quill to guard against rust.
- Touch-up chipped paintwork to keep the lathe free of rust.
- If the lathe is not to be used for some time, grease or oil it well and cover it up.

An accurate, well-engineered and quiet lathe is a delight to use.

— 3 —

LATHE ACCESSORIES

TURNING SPINDLES BETWEEN CENTRES

The following equipment will be needed for turning spindles between centres.

FOUR-PRONG DRIVE

A 9mm prong drive is usually supplied with a new lathe and is suitable for driving small spindles which have been centre-popped. In addition, a 6mm diameter, two- or four-prong drive will be useful for turning very small stock.

RING CENTRE

This accessory offers three advantages for driving a spindle over the four-prong drive. First, it is safer to use, as it has no sharp edges to catch tools or fingers; second, if a 'dig-in' occurs, the lathe will continue to revolve but the spindle will stop rotating, reducing the risk of the spindle flying off and causing an accident. Third, the centre leaves a clear ring indentation in the end of the wood, which makes it easy to remount the work accurately after removing it from the lathe for any reason. Some ring centres are sold with adjustable or removable points.

It is worth buying a good-quality ring centre because it will be used a great deal and the point can be resharpened.

LACE BOBBIN DRIVE

This drive consists of a tapered hole, square in cross section, mounted on a MT shank that will drive square spindles of 9mm and below.

FRICTION DRIVE

A four-stepped drive with an MT shank for driving spindles with pre-drilled holes of 3, 6, 10 or 16mm is extremely useful.

DRILL CHUCK

A drill chuck can be used for gripping work of a small diameter and for drilling operations in the lathe until a combination chuck is purchased. The drill chuck is not specifically designed to be used as a turning chuck in the headstock, and some of the cheaper ones are not as accurate as they should be, but when starting small-scale turning a drill chuck can be used effectively to hold small items that have a spigot. After a while, the purchase of more accurate and reliable equipment for holding both round and square stock in the headstock (*see* page 27) can be considered.

A 6mm-capacity drill chuck, fitted with a 1MT shank, is extremely useful because it is small enough not get in the way while turning. There are two drawbacks, however: because drill chucks have only three jaws, the blank needs to be turned to the round before being inserted; and the jaws have a knife-like profile, which digs in to the wood blank, and can even split it.

The drill chuck should be threaded at the back to take a ⅜in × 24tpi 1MT shank, it can then be held either in the headstock for turning small items or in the tailstock

Although designed originally for turning light pulls, the stepped friction drive has many other uses.

Small boxwood knob held by its spigot in a drill chuck, in the headstock, for turning, sanding and polishing.

for drilling. For lathes with hollow headstocks, the chuck should be used with a draw-bar screwed into the MT shank. It is not wise to use a drill chuck merely pushed into the headstock; if no tailstock support is given, the chuck can work loose. Some drill chucks will screw directly on to the headstock spindle and it is also possible to buy a drill chuck mounted on a separate carrier, which screws on to the headstock spindle. Both these options are ideal when using a lathe with a solid headstock spindle, where a draw-bar cannot be used.

The Unimat 4 has a unique thread and only the drill chuck produced exclusively for this lathe will fit. The Unimat drill chuck can be screwed directly on to the headstock or on to the tailstock spindle.

THREAD PROTECTOR

It is wise to use a thread protector screwed on to the headstock spindle when using MT accessories. The thread protector saves the spindle thread from dirt and damage and at the same time covers the thread, which can be sharp enough to cut the turner's hand. It also allows MT shanked fittings to be ejected from the headstock simply by unscrewing the protector rather than by tapping them out from the outboard end with a rod. This is kinder to the bearings and, in particular, better for small lathes, which do need to be treated with respect.

The Selbix lathe comes with a thread protector that is well engineered and rounded, with no sharp edges. Some thread protectors have a rough surface that is sharp enough to remove skin.

REVOLVING CENTRE

This centre fits in the tailstock to give support to the end of the spindle being turned. A good quality revolving centre will have a small diameter body with two bearings to cater for the radial load and one thrust race for the axial load. It is an advantage if the centre takes different points and cups; although this is a more expensive option at the start, it will prove to be a wise choice in the long term. New lathes are usually supplied with a solid

The Multistar Multi-Head revolving centre is very versatile, with its three interchangeable points, cup and faceplate. The ring centre (far right) is a separate accessory and has a removable point.

The Slimline revolving centre, manufactured by Planet, is particularly suitable for small lathes because it does not take up much room.

centre – that is, one that does not revolve and needs lubrication.

FACEPLATE TURNING

The following equipment will be required for faceplate turning.

FACEPLATE

A small 50mm diameter faceplate can be very useful for holding wood for turning without tailstock support. A wood blank screwed to the faceplate can be turned to form a jam chuck, a glue chuck and a custom-designed holding device. Because faceplates are so versatile, and relatively inexpensive, it is worth investing in a few. For miniature woodturning, you should not need to exceed 50mm diameter.

SCREWCHUCK

A small, dedicated screwchuck has a metal body threaded at one end to screw on to the headstock spindle. On the outer end there is usually a flange of about 30mm in

A 50mm faceplate (left) and (right) a faceplate with a glue chuck, coloured yellow, attached. By lining up the arrow on the glue chuck with the one permanently etched on the rim of the faceplate it is easy to put the glue chuck back on the faceplate again, confident that it will run true.

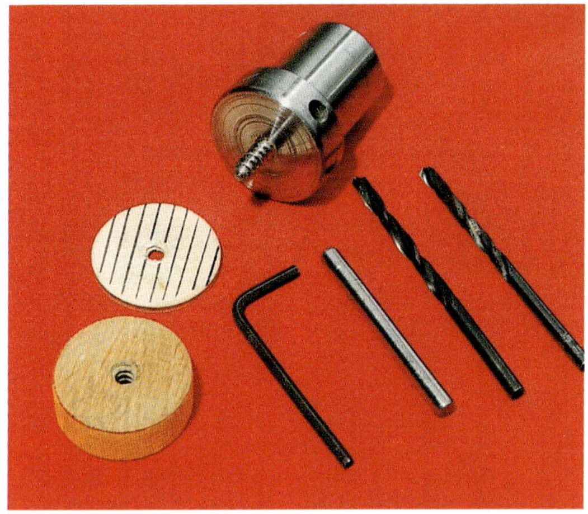

Small screwchuck, with a cross-hatched plywood spacer protecting the face. The blank in the foreground has just been removed and the thread cut by the screw is clearly visible. It is a good idea to store twist drills of the correct size with the chuck for the initial pilot holes; the larger of the two twist drills is for hardwood and the smaller for softwood.

diameter with a central hole into which a woodscrew is secured. These simple chucks are useful for turning small items such as knobs, where a central hole can be utilized to secure the knob to the host item. They are more expensive than faceplates and the quality of the screw varies with different makes. Alternatively, most combination chucks offer a screw insert as an accessory.

CHUCKING SYSTEMS

No single basic combination chuck is likely to do everything the turner wants and often it will be necessary to purchase extra sets of jaws and various accessories. Very few chucks are suitable for miniature woodturning. Although many of the larger conventional chucks offer sets of small jaws, the chucks themselves are too heavy and bulky, taking up too much room between centres and placing too much strain on the bearings of a miniature lathe. The conventional engineering scroll chuck with three or four jaws, available in small jaw sizes, is used by some woodturners. However, it is designed to be used on an engineering lathe, where it is run with a chuck guard in position. On a woodturning lathe, the unguarded chuck jaws whirr around dangerously close to the turner's fingers.

MULTISTAR MICRO CHUCK

The Multistar micro chuck has been designed specifically for miniature woodturning and, with its many accessories, is extremely accurate and versatile. This is the chuck featured throughout this book.

The body of the Multistar Micro chuck has a maximum diameter of 60mm and, with an overall length of 45mm, the chuck

The Multistar Micro chuck together with three sets of accessory jaws, a screwchuck insert, a Marlin carrier and a quick-release 1MT carrier.

The Selbix Mini Chuck with three sets of jaws and a screw insert. This is an excellent scroll chuck with a 20mm-wide protective steel safety ring covering the jaw carriers.

does not take up too much space between centres. It is indexed with twenty-four divisions and an index-locking bar is available. The chuck has no sharp edges – essential when turning miniatures, because the turner's hands are so close to the body of the chuck and the jaws.

It is not a scroll chuck. In order to change the mode from compression to expansion it is necessary to insert an expansion plug and a ring. In compression mode, it is easy to set up and usually suits all turning needs. The chuck is tightened and loosened by means of a tommy bar and a C spanner.

There are five sets of four-piece metal jaws for this chuck, which will hold round and square stock and blanks with prepared dovetail spigots. For one-off jobs, home-made wooden jaws may be used to fit in the chuck to hold blanks up to 30mm in diameter. There are two screwchuck inserts to go in this chuck, with screws of M5 and M6 diameters. These inserts are held in the chuck jaws and are ideal for holding turning blanks for small knobs, for example.

The No 1MT quick-release carrier is one of the most useful accessories, manufactured from a polycarbonate material and held in the body of the chuck to take 1MT shanked accessories without the need for a draw-bar. As the chuck is tightened, the MT shank is gripped firmly. When it is loosened, the accessory can be easily removed without having to be knocked out with a rod passed through the hollow headstock spindle. This carrier does not damage or mark the accessory, which remains in mint condition, and at the same time holds the shank very firmly so that it cannot work loose. This is particularly important when indexing.

ADDITIONAL CHUCKING DEVICES AND ACCESSORIES

Many items can be turned with a miniature lathe and the above equipment. However, as progress is made, additional chucking devices and accessories may be considered.

Mini-Grip 1000 Chuck

The Mini-Grip 1000 combination chuck was designed specifically for the small lathe by Craft Supplies and is ideally suited to it. It is available in five spindle sizes. The body has a diameter of 65mm and a length of 50mm, so it does not take

The Craft Supplies Mini-Grip 1000 chuck with small items turned in yew.

up too much distance between centres. The chuck is smooth, with no sharp edges, and it is activated by means of two C spanners. The standard jaws will compress on to a 37.5mm dovetail spigot and expand into a 65mm dovetail recess.

One of the Mini-Grip's main advantages is that no alteration needs to be made to the chuck to change it from compression to expansion and vice versa. Moreover, the accessory jaws are simply screwed on to the existing standard jaws in a quick and easy operation. There is a leeway of plus or minus 3mm for the expansion and compression modes, which is not as critical as some other chucks.

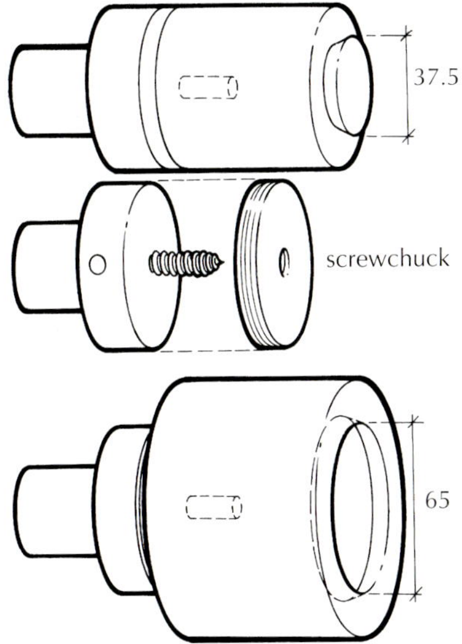

Preparing dovetail spigots and recesses for the Craft Supplies Mini-Grip 1000 chuck jaws.

The body and jaws are chemically blacked and the nickel-plated shell is drilled with twenty-four holes for indexing. There is a full range of accessories, including smaller jaws, which will be of interest to the miniaturist. This is a very good chuck for turning small boxes, bowls and vases (*see* the picture above), but perhaps less versatile than the Multistar Micro for really tiny work.

The APTC Junior Collet Chuck

The Junior collet chuck measures 68mm in overall length, with a body diameter of 55mm and an extended nose diameter of 30mm. The metal parts are smooth and it is safe to use when turning miniature items. The chuck backplate is secured by means of four hex bolts and other threaded backplates are available. This well-designed and well-engineered chuck takes high-quality metal engineering collets in a range of 1 to 13mm capacity;

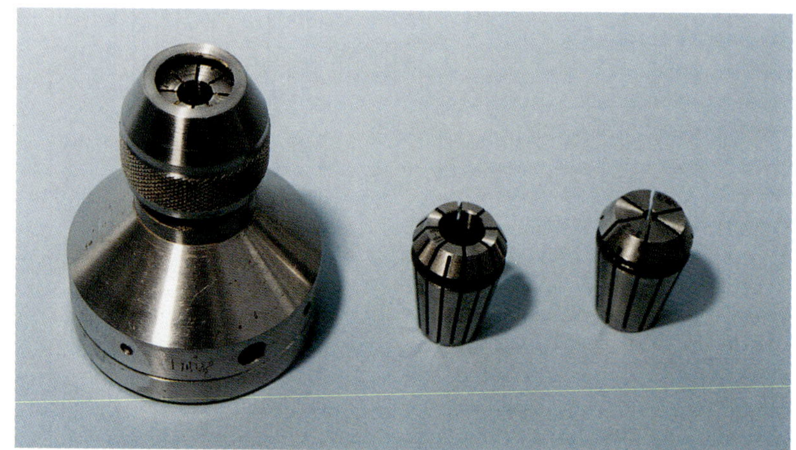

APTC Junior collet chuck with three precision steel collets.

The APTC collet chuck is smooth, with no sharp edges. Because the Little Gem has a hollow headstock spindle and the collet chuck is hollow throughout, long lengths of wood can be passed from the rear of the headstock and held in the collet, with just the required length protruding for turning.

these can be purchased separately. For miniature work, the 10, 6 and 3mm collets will be the most useful. When turning items of a very small diameter, it is best to use 6mm stock in the 6mm collet and turn the outboard end of the wood down to the desired diameter, rather than use a smaller collet and risk vibration and breakage.

Each collet has a number of machined slits in the body, which allow it to compress on a square or a round blank and spring open when the chuck is released. The collet is inserted into the front of the chuck body and the knurled nose cone is tightened by hand to compress it on to the blank. The bore of the collet is 31mm long and this provides a really positive hold on the blank.

The secret of success when using collet chucks lies in the accurate preparation of the blank to the correct parallel size. This chuck is hollow throughout, which has the advantage of allowing long lengths of wood to be passed through the chuck, and through a hollow headstock, for repetitive work such as turning batches of small knobs.

Multistar Compact Titan Scroll Chuck

The Multistar Micro chuck is too small to be threaded for larger spindle diameters; its bigger brother, the Duplex, is more suitable and has a similar wide selection of jaws, together with a carrier that will take the Marlin range. Multistar has recently introduced the four-jaw Compact Titan scroll chuck, suitable for the larger lathe. It can be used on the Carbatec MkII and the Selbix Mini, but it is too large for some of the smaller miniature lathes, including the Tyme Little Gem. The Titan is also an excellent choice for full-sized turning.

The chuck body has a patented safety ring to protect the turner from the carriers on to which the jaws are fitted, making it an extremely safe chuck to use. An accessory mount can be fitted to this chuck to take the Marlin range. (Note: this range of accessories can also be screwed on to a MT carrier, which can be fitted directly into the headstock spindle in the lathe; this is obviously a cheaper option. *See* page 32 for details.)

There are a number of jaws but two sets are particularly interesting for small-scale work. The TCJ015 finger jaws hold wood from just under 3mm to just over 13mm, round or square, and are ideal for holding small blanks for spindle work. Because the chuck is hollow, long lengths of stock can be passed through a hollow headstock and through the back of the chuck and there are times when it is very useful to be able to do this. The smooth, tapered fingers grip extremely well and allow excellent access to the work.

The TCJ075 jaws are the standard, workhorse jaws of the system, expanding into a 75mm dovetail and contracting on to a 50mm dovetail spigot, and can be used for turning bowls and platters. For miniature turning, these jaws will be used predominantly for holding home-made glue chucks.

The Marlin accessory mount should also be considered. This is screwed

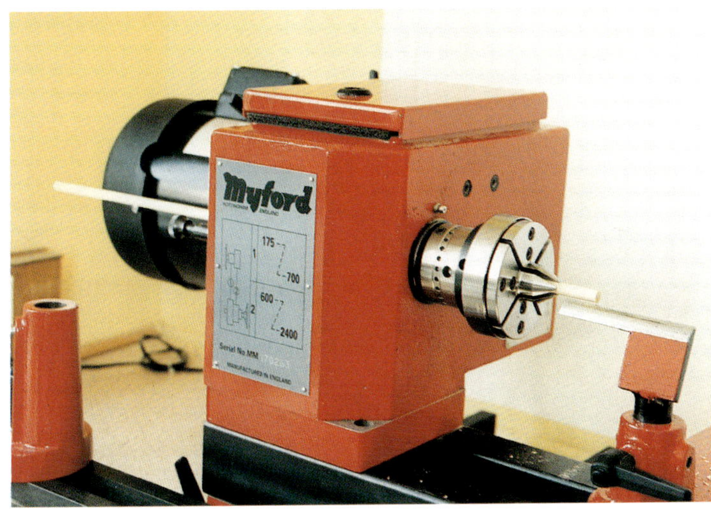

Turning miniatures on a large lathe such as the Myford Mystro. The Titan 'finger jaws' are gripping a length of dowel passed right through the hollow headstock. The chuck and jaws are designed so that there are no sharp edges.

directly to the chuck body for greatest rigidity and accuracy, although it can be held in the standard TCJ075 jaws if preferred. The fact that the mount will take the Marlin range (*see below*) offers a huge range of possibilities.

MULTISTAR MARLIN SYSTEM

The Marlin system can be used in addition to, or instead of, the Micro chuck. It is a good idea to start with the chuck and some of the accessories mentioned above, and to think later about adding the Marlin system. The MT shank and the various screw-on accessories of this range take up little room on the lathe. The overall diameter of the various accessories is very small and the turner is not impeded when carrying out intricate work on a miniature scale. The collet chuck, which is part of the system, is particularly effective for holding square or round micro-sized blanks.

Basically, the system consists of a MT shank, which is placed directly into the headstock spindle on to which various interchangeable accessories are fitted. The MT shank is threaded externally (½in × 20tpi) at the outboard end to accept the range of accessories and internally (M5) to accept various Marlin centrepoints. The shank has a radial hole and a tommy bar to make it easy to screw and unscrew the various heads. It is available in MT sizes 1, 2 and 3, and in two different forms:

1. Solid at the narrow end for headstocks that are not drilled throughout.
2. Drilled and tapped M5 to take a draw-bar and cone nut. This type is suitable for headstocks that are drilled throughout. The draw-bar and cone nut ensure that the MT shank does not work loose from the headstock spindle during use. The threaded rod draw-bar is supplied in 300mm lengths and can be cut to suit individual lathes.

The Marlin accessory mount screwed on to the chuck body holding the collet chuck. The modified toolrest allows the fingers of the left hand to be used to steady the very small spindle, which is being turned with a micro oval skew. There are no sharp edges on the chuck, jaws or collet – this is very important when working so close to the wood being turned.

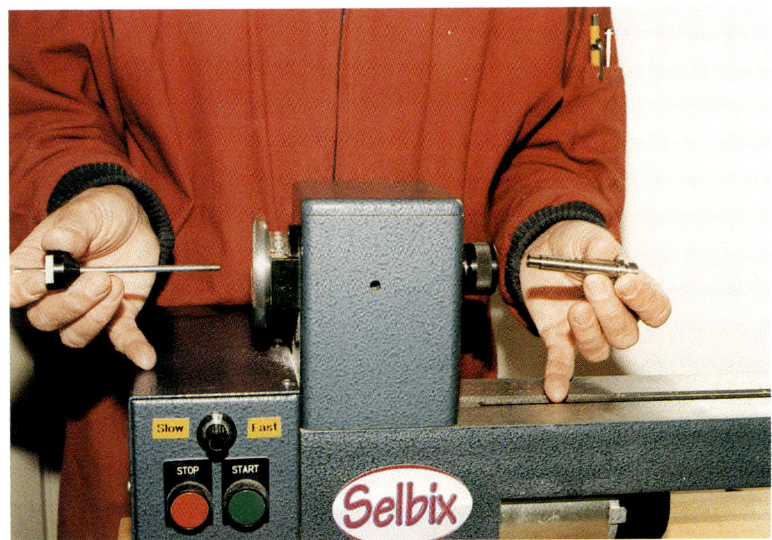

A threaded draw-bar is passed through the outboard end of the headstock and screwed into the end of the inserted MT carrier, to prevent it working loose. Once the carrier is fitted, any of the Marlin accessories can be screwed to it.

The second form may be used with headstocks that are not drilled throughout but the shank will need to be held in the quick-release MT carrier held in the Micro chuck.

Surprisingly few woodturners are familiar with the Marlin system, which is unique and comprehensive. Although the system provides scope for driving and holding work of *all* sizes, it is worth explaining in detail how the various drives, drill chucks, faceplates and collet holder may be used for small-scale work.

Note: it is advisable always to use the thread protector, to reduce the risk of damaging the headstock spindle thread and to aid the ejection of MT fittings.

FOUR-PRONG DRIVE

There are several four-prong drives, in various sizes; the 6mm and the 12mm are often the most useful for small-scale work. The drive is supplied with a silver steel centrepoint threaded at one end (M5) and a small nut, which allows the point to be adjusted beyond the blades. For softwoods, the point can be used in the extended position and for hardwoods it can be shortened. These centre pins can be resharpened or replaced if necessary.

The pin is fitted first and then the drive head is screwed on to the ½in × 20tpi end

The 6mm four-prong drive about to be screwed on to the carrier. The pin can be adjusted in length and can be reground if the point becomes blunt or damaged, or completely replaced at very little cost. The blades of the drive can be kept sharp by honing. This is one of the smallest four-prong drives and is very useful indeed.

of the MT shank. A 19mm wide spanner flat on the body of the drive makes it easy to tighten and remove. This is a lovely drive for small spindle work, produced in tempered British tool steel to give a combination of hardness and toughness. The prongs can be reconditioned with a diamond file.

The 25mm diameter screwchuck screws directly to the carrier. The plywood spacer, coloured red, protects the body of the chuck from damage. The screw's sharp point has been ground off.

FACEPLATE

The 45mm diameter faceplate has three countersunk holes to take No 6 woodscrews. Filing a register mark on the outer rim of the faceplates ensures that any rechucked work is repositioned accurately (as long as the blank has been similarly marked). This small faceplate may be used for glue chucking, jam chucking and as a pressure pad (*see* pages 70, 71 and 74 for more information on the techniques).

SCREWCHUCK

The very small screwchuck has an overall body diameter of 25mm. The chuck has a Riesser M5, high-strength screw, which is secured by means of a hex screw in the side of the body. Care needs to be taken when fitting the Riesser screw, so that it is not misaligned. This chuck also has a spanner flat to assist mounting and removal. A 4mm-thick plywood spacer will avoid inadvertently damaging the face of the chuck and you could also grind off the sharp point of the end of the screw, which often draws blood! This screwchuck is fine for turning little knobs and finials for restoration work, where a screw hole in the back of the piece is acceptable.

The Marlin carrier and screwchuck held in the Micro chuck fitted with the quick-release carrier. A small vase has been turned from a blank mounted on the screwchuck and is about to be parted off. The Micro chuck can be left on the headstock spindle most of the time and the carrier inserted for the use of MT-shanked accessories.

COLLET CHUCK

The collet chuck screws directly on to the ½in × 20tpi end of the MT shank. It comes with eight glass-filled polymide collets, which hold a range of 0 to 6mm diameter

A very small square spindle held securely in a collet. A micro chess piece is being turned, and there is no risk of vibration and there will be enough wood left in the collet to turn a second piece.

stock, making it particularly useful for the modeller working on a micro scale. The glass-filled polymide collets are strong and accurate, and will not mark the work. They are fitted by unscrewing the knurled nose cone by hand, placing the collet in the body and replacing the cone; finger tightening is sufficient.

All the collets, with the exception of the smallest, have four jaws, allowing carefully prepared square blanks to be held, as well as round stock. They will also hold small drills, burrs and grinding and polishing heads (of which there is an enormous choice), and the chuck can be mounted in the tailstock for drilling, too.

Woodturners attracted to small-scale work often have an engineering background and are used to working with accuracy and precision, and patience. For this kind of work it pays to spend time preparing the wood (*see* page 48); for example, square-section blanks to be held in a collet chuck must be *absolutely* square to start with.

This collet chuck is more suitable for small-scale work than a conventional Jacob's-type drill chuck for the following reasons:

- Its overall diameter is only 22mm and it therefore does not get in the way when turning micro items.
- The collets are four-jaw, allowing square blanks to be held.
- The glass-filled polymide collets do not crush or mark the wood.
- The collets give a very positive grip on very small items.

Select your accessories wisely, look after them carefully and they will serve you well.

— 4 —

TURNING TOOLS

MINIATURE TOOLS

What is meant by the term 'miniature' turning tool? Somewhat confusingly, there is no common standard.

'Miniature' turning tools are usually 250mm long overall, with handles measuring 150mm and 100mm blades. Several firms manufacture this size of tool but others label their chisels, scrapers and gouges as 'miniature' when in fact they exceed these dimensions. Others describe such tools as 'micro' when they are in fact miniature. The best tools are scaled-down versions of full-size turning tools and the same amount of work goes into their manufacture. Many of them are produced by experienced toolmakers, with an impressive attention to detail and the result is a safe, reliable tool that will give many years of service. Manufacturers such as Ashley Iles, Crown, Hamlet, Henry Taylor and Sorby can all be relied upon to produce good quality high-speed steel (HSS) blades.

FIRST TOOLS

The following list represents a good selection of miniature turning tools to start with:

- 12.5mm oval skew chisel
- 8mm skew chisel
- 4mm beading tool
- 6mm spindle gouge
- 2.5mm parting tool
- 6mm round-nosed scraper

A roughing-out gouge will also be required. The miniature versions do not perform well, however, and a standard 13mm tool will be more satisfactory. A large, thin parting tool, rather similar to a knife, is also recommended.

Other, more specialist tools can be added over time; these are described throughout this book.

It is possible to buy one set of miniatures to serve all needs, but it is better to buy the tools separately. Sets often contain one or more tools, that are not required.

HIGH-SPEED STEEL (HSS)

High-speed steel (HSS) tools are specifically designed and manufactured for the miniature turner and are suitable for work on a wide range of items.

In the past, the blades of turning tools were made from carbon steel but today almost all of them are produced in M2 high-speed steel (HSS). HSS blades keep their cutting edge six times longer than those made from carbon steel. They can be ground on a 150mm drystone grinder, or on a sanding disc. No liquid or oil is necessary, and the risk of adversely affecting the heat treatment given to the steel by the manufacturer is greatly reduced.

CUSTOMIZING TOOLS

Many turners have a preference for a custom-shaped handle. For example, I reduce the length of Ashley Iles handles to 115mm and re-drill the tang hole to a greater depth, so that the blades are only 65mm long. This modification can make the tool fit more neatly in the hand and help the turner to achieve better control.

To shorten the handles, first knock the blade out. Mount the ferrule end in the headstock and support the other end with a revolving centre. Using a spindle gouge, turn the end of the handle to reduce it to the length required. Sand and polish and re-insert the blade.

Ashley Iles will supply tools with a shorter handle if this is requested when ordering. Blades and brass ferrules can also be bought separately and mounted on to hand-turned handles.

MAINTENANCE

STORAGE

After investing a considerable sum of money in turning tools, it is worth taking the time and trouble to fit out a box to store them. In this way, cutting edges will be protected, and your fingers are less likely to be damaged than if you are rummaging around in a bag or a pile of shavings. Discipline yourself to put each tool away after use in its allotted space. The simple plywood box (*see* the picture on page 11) is fitted out to take chisels, gouges and scrapers, callipers and ceramic tile, together with other small accessories.

KEEPING TOOLS SHARP

It is most important to keep cutting edges sharp; blunt tools do not produce good results. Newly purchased chisels and gouges will have been ground to the correct angle and will need just a little gentle honing to provide a keen cutting edge. A Spyderco ceramic stone, made in the USA of high alumina ceramic, is ideal for honing. Particles of alumina, or man-made sapphires, are mixed with a special ceramic bonding agent and then compressed at very high pressures and fired in kilns for up to three days. The result is a

Grinding a 12.5mm oval skew on a sanding disc mounted in a drill chuck on the Unimat.

stone that is capable of cutting any metal, will not wear out and will remain absolutely flat. It is used dry, so there is no need for oil or water, and it can be cleaned with a household cleaner, scrubbed with a nylon nailbrush and rinsed with water. The medium-grade tile, which measures 200 × 50mm wide, is recommended. There are also small-section slipstones, which are ideal for removing the wire edge on the inside of gouges.

Honing Skews, Beading Tools and Parting Tools

Place the bevel flat on a ceramic stone and hold it down firmly with a forefinger. Draw the tool back and repeat the process several times until a wire edge is formed on the upper edge of the bevel. Turn the blade over and repeat the same process until a burr forms on the upper edge.

Repeat the action each side until the wire edge breaks off, leaving a new sharp cutting edge. Moving the blade backwards and forwards may cause the forming of a convex or rounded bevel, which is not desirable; moreover, it is easy to nick the finger on the forward stroke.

Honing a skew on a ceramic tile.

Honing Gouges and Rounded Scrapers

This is more difficult. The inside of the gouge flute can be honed with a shaped ceramic stone, remembering to keep the stone flat in the flute, to avoid the inside edge becoming rounded. One option is to make a shaped wooden honing stick, formed exactly to the shape of the inside flute of the chisel, and covered with cloth-backed abrasive.

Using a Sanding Disc for Sharpening

Blades that are honed regularly will seldom need to be reground. If regrinding is necessary, use a sanding disc rather than a bench grinder, which can be too aggressive; the blades are very small and the grinder may take away too much metal.

A home-made sanding disc can be made by securing a round disc of MDF, or plywood, to a faceplate and turning it to a diameter of about 75mm. Use the toolrest (*see* the picture on page 37) or a small table to rest the tool on, with a stem to go in the toolrest holder. Aluminium oxide 120-grit abrasive paper can be glued to the MDF or plywood to produce a firm sanding disc, which can be used directly in the lathe for regrinding when required. When the abrasive wears out, just glue on a new piece.

Ashley Iles offers to regrind tools purchased from them. Simply telephone for details if you need to use this service, which is free of charge.

Safety: *always* wear eye protection when carrying out any grinding operation.

USING THE TOOLS

It takes time to acquire the skills and techniques required to use the tools well; some will prove to be more difficult to master than others, but perseverance will yield just rewards. The objective is to

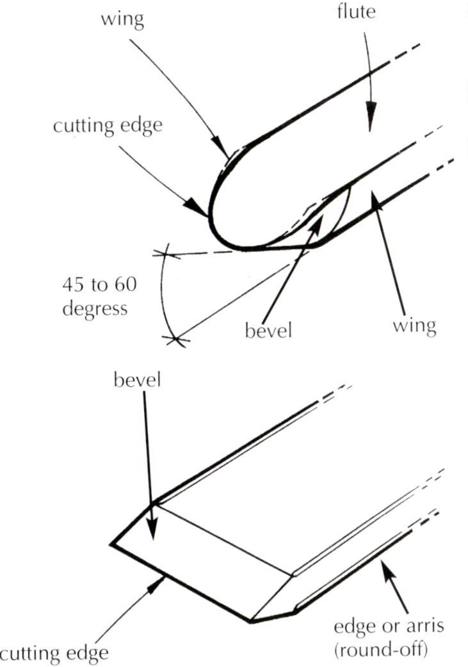

Parts of turning tools.

learn how to use the tools so that they *cut* rather than *scrape* the wood. The cut should produce crisp detail. This is the hallmark of good turning and, although a little sanding will be needed, it can be destroyed by over-zealous sanding.

Once they have been honed, newly purchased tools are ready for use. Each tool is designed for a specific task and needs a particular technique.

Roughing-Out Gouge

The roughing-out gouge is used for turning down a rough blank to the desired diameter. The difference between the roughing-out gouge and the spindle

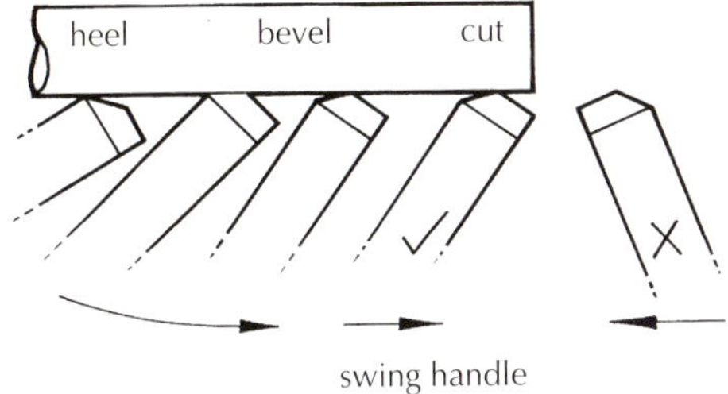

Roughing-out gouge.

Starting to turn a rough blank to the round on the Rexon miniature lathe, using the roughing-out gouge. Note the position of the tool.

gouge is that the wings of the spindle gouge are ground well back, whereas the end of the roughing-out gouge, when viewed from above, is virtually straight across.

Technique:

1. Hold the bottom of the handle in the right hand – the 'control hand' – and rest the tool on the toolrest. Steady the tool on the rest with the left hand – the 'steady hand'.
2. Bring the heel of the tool on to the surface of the wood and swing the handle until the bevel is parallel to the wood and rubbing against it.
3. Swing the handle further round until the cutting edge begins to cut, but the bevel is still supporting the tool.
4. Move the tool forward, maintaining the angle with the wood, so that a cylindrical cut is made.
5. Go *off* the end of a spindle, not *into* it.
6. Repeat the cuts until the required diameter is achieved. A number of gentle cuts is better than one deep one.
7. Keep the handle down – do not let it come up.

Spindle Gouge

The spindle gouge is the most useful shaping tool and is primarily used to form a cylinder, curve, cove, bead, V cut or a chamfer on spindles, knobs, finials, and so on. It is also used for hollowing out and shaping small bowls, platters and goblets. The more intricate the shape, the smaller the tool required. The first gouge to master is the 6mm; subsequently, further gouges, down to 4mm, may be considered.

Technique:

1. When preparing to cut, bring the heel into contact with the wood, swing the handle to give bevel contact and then swing slightly more to commence cutting. If the turner goes in with the cutting edge first, the tool will start cutting too soon.
2. Use the tool on its side with the flute pointing in the direction of the cut and with the bevel close to the wood; keep the handle down.
3. When turning hollows a scooping action is required to keep the bevel rubbing.
4. Always cut from large to small diameter – never cut 'uphill'.
5. When cutting a V, or commencing a cove, start with the edges of both flutes pointing vertically.
6. When producing beads a rolling action is needed, with the tool ending up on its side.

Skew Chisel

The skew is used for shaping spindles and beads, and so on, for cutting Vs and for cleaning up the end grain on spindles. There are two sorts of skew: the type made from conventional rectangular-section steel and the one produced from oval-section (the 'oval skew'). Both types are used in exactly the same way; the picture below shows an oval skew in use.

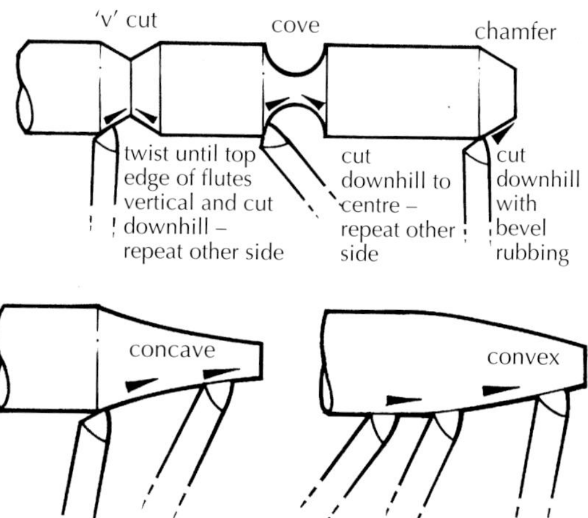

Using the spindle gouge.

The oval shape tends to be easier to control and the edges of the blade do not catch on the toolrest. The sharp edges of a standard rectangular skew may be rounded off using a slipstone, to prevent the tool dragging on the toolrest.

The skew is difficult to master, but it will give extremely fine finishes and prove to be the most useful tool for spindle turning. Patience and perseverance are vital.

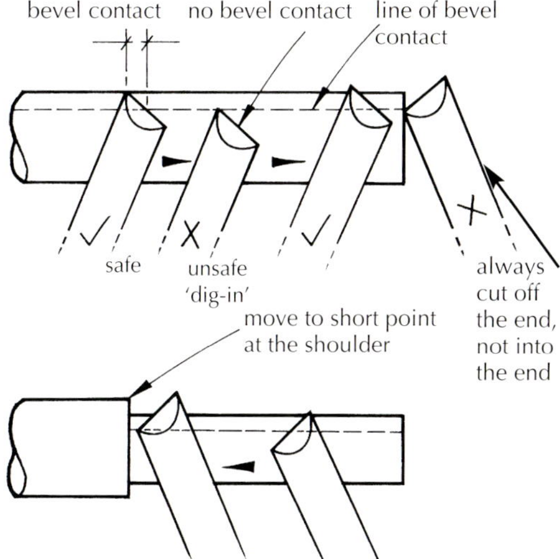

Skew chisel.

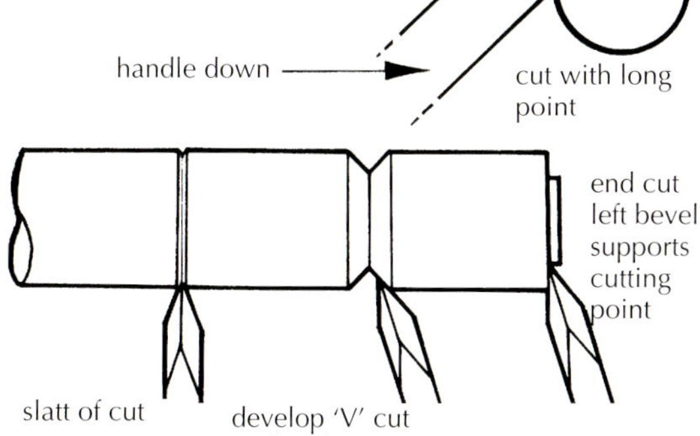

Using the oval skew chisel.

Technique:

1. When preparing to cut, approach the wood with the heel, swing the handle to allow the bevel to rub and then swing slightly to allow the cutting edge to cut.
2. Use the long point to form V cuts.
3. Avoid the point digging in.
4. Turn 'off the end' not 'on to the end'.
5. Move to the short point when making shoulders.
6. Use the long point to tidy up the ends of spindles.
7. Swing the handle to form the curve but only cut 'downhill'.
8. Keep the bevel close to the wood.
9. Keep the handle down.

Parting Tool

A thin parting tool is used for very fine work, cutting deep grooves and parting off wood. The end of one 2.5mm parting tool blade may be ground to a thin section of 1mm. The standard 2.5mm blade is used for turning spigots.

Position of the hands and fingers when using the oval skew to turn a small spindle. The left thumb holds the blade down, to produce a planing cut.

Technique:
1. Start with the bevel rubbing and the handle down; as the cut commences, bring the handle up and push the point into the wood.
2. Keep the tool vertical and square to the wood.
3. Do not cut right through a revolving piece of work; leave 6mm and cut through the remainder of the wood with a fine handsaw and with the lathe stationary.
4. For deep cuts, widen the cut to reduce friction and heat.
5. Take care when re-entering a groove already started because it is easy to catch the sides.

Beading Tool

The beading tool has a square-section blade and is wider than the parting tool. It is used for heavier work such as forming wider spigots but it can also be used for rolling beads, hollowing out the bottoms of boxes and for turning synthetic materials.

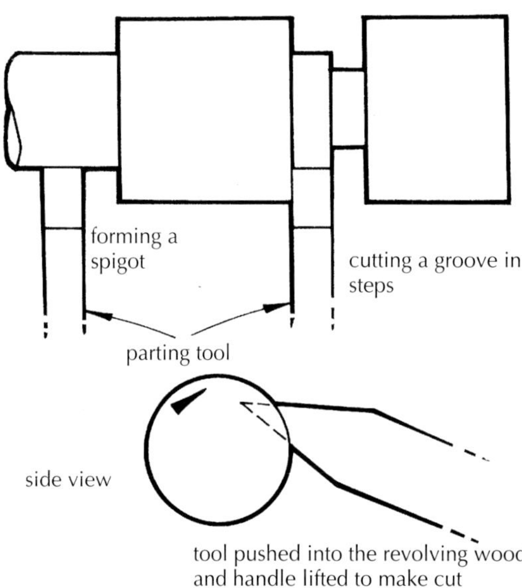

Using the parting tool.

Technique:

The beading tool can be used as a skew chisel or as a parting tool and the technique is the same.

The Scraper

The scraper is used for finishing flat or curved surfaces in faceplate work and for smoothing the inside of bowls and platters. The scraper should not be used for spindle turning.

Technique:
1. Keep the handle up with the cutting edge slightly down.
2. Take light cuts only.

Armrest

The armrest consists of a straight 380mm long handle with a 180mm blade made from 6mm thick steel. The top surface, by the ferrule, is 12mm wide, tapering to 6mm at the end, which turns up to form a hook; this stops the tool slipping off the end of the rest.

The armrest takes some getting used to, but it is worth persevering. It allows the turner to work with great sensitivity and gives precise control of the tool against the piece, so that the best possible finish

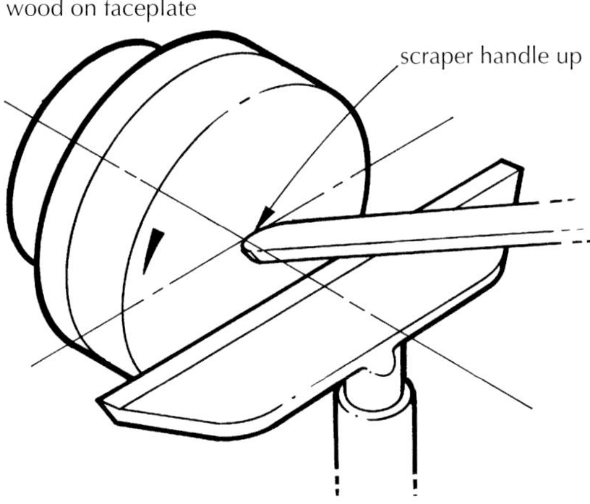

Using the scraper.

The armrest with its long handle.

can be achieved. The armrest is used when turning small items, for the end of a blank, rather than the sides – a typical example would be turning the ball end of a Staunton chess pawn. It is also ideal when turning and gently shaping artificial materials and boxwood mounted on the faceplate.

Technique:

1. First, set the toolrest parallel with the axis of the lathe.
2. Hold the handle under the armpit, with the hooked end resting on the toolrest. The turning tool is held in the right hand with the thumb and forefinger stretched along the blade.
3. Place the left hand with the thumb pressing down on the tool and the lower fingers curled round the toolrest stem under the tool.
4. By moving the body, the position of the tool cutting edge against the work can be altered very slightly, allowing really sensitive and flowing cuts to be made.

MICRO TURNING TOOLS

Micro HSS tools are made by only a few toolmakers. The set featured in this book is manufactured in Sheffield by Crown and can be purchased with either fixed blades or double-ended adjustable blades. With the latter, the turner can alter the blade to the exact length required and each end can be ground differently.

These tools have been designed specifically for modellers who want to carry out intricate work. The 120mm handles fit

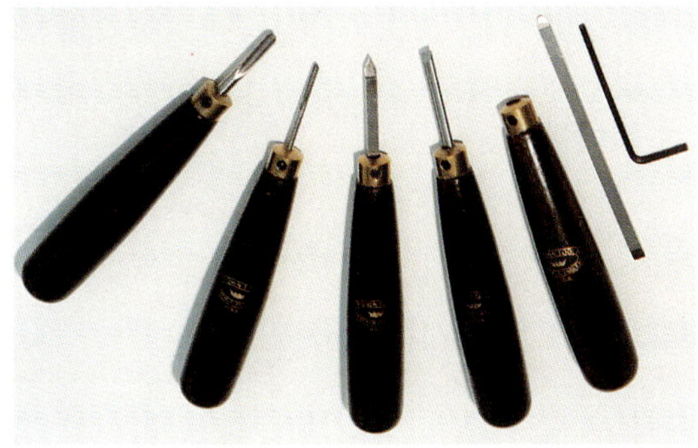

Micro turning tools.

comfortably into the hand and the length of the blade is altered by means of a grub screw in the ferrule. If the blade will not go far enough into the handle, simply drill the hole deeper. For most turning a maximum of 30mm of blade extending from the handle is recommended, to negate any risk of the blade flexing.

The five tools in the set are as follows:

- Oval skew 4.35mm wide
- Spindle gouge 2mm round stock
- Spindle gouge 4mm round stock
- Scraper (round at one end and square at the other) 4.5mm wide
- Parting tool 2mm thick

To keep the gouges sharp, use a sanding disc rather than a grinder, otherwise too much metal may be removed. For the other tools, honing on a ceramic stone will keep them really sharp.

The basic technique is to hold the tool handle in the right hand and use the left hand with the thumb over the tool to keep it on the toolrest. The forefinger is held under the work, particularly in the case of a spindle, to act as a steady. For more on technique, *see* pages 136, and the information on turning very tiny objects.

Always keep turning tools sharp. Do not dither – be firm and positive.

Suggested modifications to tools:

Oval skew	Grind one end square across and leave the other at a skew angle
Gouges	Grind one end with the wings well back
Scraper	Produce a double bevel on both the round and the square end, to reduce the risk of the tool digging in
Parting tool	Reduce the thickness to 1mm at one end of the blade for a length of 10mm to produce a really thin parting tool for delicate work

— 5 —

MATERIALS

WOOD

Woodturners are often prepared to spend freely on lathes and equipment but many begrudge having to buy wood. A few decades ago, timber was expensive and the choice was very limited. Today, however, turners are spoilt for choice. Part of the appeal of small-scale turning is that it requires relatively small pieces of timber. Generally, two types of wood are used: decorative woods for small pieces such as bud vases, boxes, bowls and jewellery, and fine-grain woods for highly detailed and scaled work.

DECORATIVE WOODS

Home-grown woods such as yew can give dramatic and artistic results when turned and even branchwood can be used with great success. Even laburnum and plum from the garden can be used, with delightful results. Sometimes disaster strikes and the wood cracks, but very little expenditure has been incurred. It is always worth having a go because that is half the fun of woodturning.

There are also many exotic woods with striking grain and colour that can be purchased.

Occasionally, a particular type of wood can cause an allergic reaction and needs to be marked down as one to avoid in future.

A selection of highly decorative imported woods.

Home-grown yew in log and plank form.

FINE-GRAIN WOODS

Very fine, skilfully made models are sometimes spoilt because the grain of the wood used is out of scale. Although the finished piece might need staining, and even if the item is to be painted, a fine-grain hardwood is almost always a better bet, and more likely to look 'right'. Modellers producing small-scale furniture, for example, often mistakenly believe that an exact copy can only be made using the same wood as the full-sized piece. Oak may have been used for a full-sized table, but this wood will not look right in a dolls' house because the size of the grain will be inappropriate.

Boxwood, lemonwood, holly, sycamore, pear and ebony are all suitable for modelling; they are stable to turn, carve, route and sand and take a very good finish. Some modellers use jelutong or lime, but these timbers are rather soft and prone to damage, although lime is excellent for carving. Ramin is often sold as modelling wood but it tends to splinter and not everyone finds it pleasant to use. Ebony turns, burnishes and polishes very well and can be used to simulate iron gun barrels, for example. It is readily available; search for the really black wood and avoid pieces that are disappointingly brown. Alternatively, use a wood such as pear and stain it to represent ebony.

Timber recovered from old furniture should not be discounted. However, while some of the early Cuban mahogany, with its very fine grain and almost brown colour, can be used to very good effect, modern mahogany can be disappointing. It is also best to avoid pine completely, unless it is the old, yellow wood that was used by pattern makers.

Wood is not the only material that can be turned. Bone was used by French prisoners of war during the Napoleonic period to make very fine models, some of which are still on display in museums. Ivory was very widely used in the past for finials and chess pieces. Today, some very good modern substitutes for these materials exist, in the form of cast polyester resin (*see* page 76).

BOXWOOD

This excellent wood has always been the chosen wood for the very finest models and is nearly always used for model ships of museum quality. It has a very fine grain and can be easily cut, drilled, shaped, stained, painted and polished. English boxwood is particularly suitable because it has a lovely colour and an extremely fine grain.

With all woods, there are many different varieties of the same species and it is essential to pick and choose carefully. Boxwood can sometimes be found at a sawmill in log or branch form and a small quantity can be made to go a long way. Any offer of good quality boxwood should be snapped up, even if it is not to be used immediately. It will store happily under cover for years. Seal the ends of boxwood lengths that will not be used for some time and check and restack stock at least twice a year.

Blanks for miniature woodturning prepared from box branchwood. The timber has been thicknessed and planed and cut into accurate small blanks with the Unimat saw accessory.

A thick branch of boxwood like this, with its distinctive bark, is probably several hundred years old. It is safer to cut branchwood with a hand saw.

Lemonwood from Central and South America is a very useful substitute for European boxwood. The timber is hard, tough and durable with a uniform texture, giving an excellent smooth finish on turning.

DOWELLING

Bamboo barbecue skewers, toothpicks and table mats are easily converted into very useful dowelling. Small spigots turned on the end of a spindle tend to be very fragile, so use thin bamboo dowel in diameters of 1 or 2mm to glue into the spindle and into the host hole. The result is a strong and durable bond. Metals will cause corrosion in time but the bamboo is in sympathy with the wood and does the job beautifully.

Two nutcrackers turned in boxwood, a wood that was once used extensively for items of household treen because of its strength and durability.

SOURCES

SPECIALIST RETAILERS

Buying suitable wood from a specialist supplier is no problem. The price of prepared timber may be high, but the accurately prepared blanks have been selected, seasoned and cut, from rough planks, and the machining is an expensive process. Retailers specializing in woodturning products stock a wide range of both home-grown and imported hardwoods. They also sell packs of wood ready cut and prepared for turning lace bobbins or pens, which can be useful.

It is more satisfactory to visit the retailer and choose the wood in person, but if this is not possible many companies also offer a mail order service. The catalogues are usually informative and show the breadth of the choice.

OTHER SOURCES

Some timber suppliers are more used to supplying large quantities of rough-sawn timber for woodwork and joinery, and may not be able to help turners who need a small amount of wood. A local furniture maker or joiner, on the other hand, may offer for sale offcuts of seasoned hardwood, which can be very useful and inexpensive.

Woods such as holly, hawthorn, spindle, fruitwoods and boxwood can be collected from the hedgerow or garden, then cut and seasoned to produce modelling timber. The results can be either successful or very disappointing. It is a slow process, requiring at least one year for each inch of thickness, and sometimes the wood cracks badly before or after it has been turned. However, if there is a good source of green wood, and somewhere under cover to dry it, it is worth having a try. It is most satisfying to produce a turned item from wood cut and seasoned from the garden.

PREPARING WOOD

It is vital to spend time preparing timber accurately before beginning work and it makes sense to prepare stock in one session ready for later work. This way, it is easy to assess the stock levels and the timber can be stored neatly in prepared batches.

Getting the wood to the right thickness for miniature work requires patience. If blanks are prepared carefully, precious timber will not be wasted; less wood will be removed on the lathe and less dust and fewer shavings will be created. As a bonus, turning tools will need sharpening less often, and there is less risk of miniature lathes being damaged, which may happen if large, irregular-shaped blanks are mounted ready for turning.

BY HAND

Equipment needed:

- A vice or clamp to hold the wood on to a bench or saw-horse while it is being worked on.
- An inexpensive general-purpose 20in hardpoint saw for rip and crosscutting. (These saws have hardened teeth, which cannot be resharpened but do last quite a long time. Grandad's beautiful but rusty old saw will not do! Modern tools, with their superior steel, are more efficient and make jobs much easier).
- A smoothing plane to reduce the thickness of the wood and to prepare a smooth surface.
- A mitre saw, consisting of a jig and saw, to true up the ends accurately; these are easy to use and give excellent results; alternatively, use a 20tpi gents brass-backed saw.
- A cabinet scraper, for smoothing wood.

BY MACHINE

The bandsaw will prove to be the most useful machine for cutting lots of wood quickly and easily. Although a bandsaw still needs to be treated with great respect, it is a safer machine to use than a circular saw and more versatile. Of the two basic types – the two-wheel and three-wheel – the former is reliable and easier to use. The space and budget available will determine the size of machine chosen; go for the largest and best quality machine you can afford.

The bandsaw should have an adjustable fence that is capable of being calibrated, otherwise it will not cut straight. To cut straight lengths and thin sections, the machine should be fitted with a blade 9mm wide, or more; for cutting roughly shaped round blanks ready for turning, the blade will need to be less than 9mm.

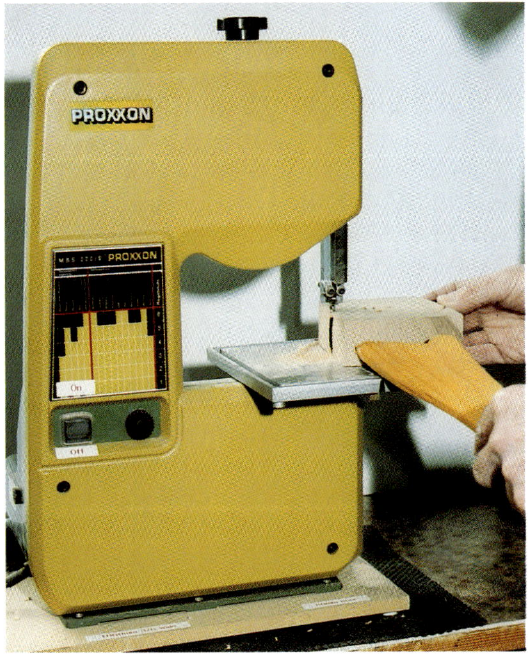

Cutting a blank on a small Proxxon two-wheel bandsaw, using a push-stick to guide the wood. The narrow blade cuts small round blanks up to 50mm thick. Although excellent in every other way, this bandsaw does not have a fence, so a home-made one is cramped to the saw table when cutting spindle blanks.

Safety: great care needs to be taken when operating a bandsaw, especially when cutting small pieces of wood. Keep fingers well away from the blade and *always* use a push-stick. When cutting really small sections, glue the wood temporarily to a larger piece of wood before passing it through the saw.

Once the timber has been cut it can be put through a thicknesser/planer that is designed to produce sections down to about 6mm thick. If the wood is temporarily fixed with double-sided tape to a piece of 18mm MDF, 250mm wide and 450mm long, it is possible to produce thin sections. The blades need to be sharp and accurately set, otherwise there is a tendency for the machine to chew up the wood.

A thicknesser is a rather expensive luxury, but a simple and cheaper alternative is to use a drum sander in a bench drill or with a power drill in a drillstand. The sanders are fitted with 12mm spindles to fit most bench drills and are available in four diameters. All four sizes take 75mm wide abrasive, which is clamped into a slot in the side of the drum and then locked tightly. The manufacturers recommend spindle speeds of between 750rpm and 1,750rpm according to timber species. On small sections, or expensive timbers, power sanding saves wood. Sawing a little over the finished required size, and then sanding eliminates the need to plane. Start with a coarse grit, then use increasingly fine grades until the finish is satisfactory.

A purpose-made jig (*see* the picture below) will make an effective small thicknesser. This jig is designed to fit any size of bench drill and the 10mm diameter holes can be spaced to suit a specific drill table. The distance between the outside of the drum and the fence is adjusted by swivelling the table. The hole in the

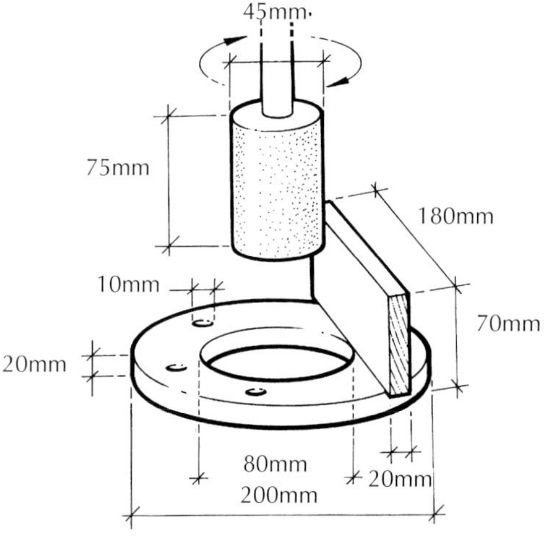

Jig for sanding drum thicknesser.

centre enables the drum to be lowered slightly below the level of the jig. A great deal of dust is produced, so a mask is essential and some form of dust extraction, or a heavyweight vacuum cleaner collecting as much dust as possible, would be sensible.

Do not press the wood against the drum, let the abrasive do the work and aim to remove only a small amount with each pass, repeating passes until the required thickness is achieved. Make sure that the piece of wood being put through the sander is at least 300mm long, as shorter pieces are too difficult to handle. It is vital that the permanently fitted fence is at right-angles to the base.

FINISHING

Finishing the turned piece to a satisfactory standard requires a high level of patience.

SANDING

A cloth-backed abrasive, sold by the metre on a roll, is more comfortable to hold than other versions. It is also very flexible. No matter how many times it is folded, in order to get into nooks and crannies, it will not crack. This type of abrasive can even be washed when it becomes clogged, and reused many times. Grits of 240, 320 and 400 will be most suitable for small-scale work. For a very fine finish, on woods such as boxwood and on synthetic materials, the Micromesh range has grits ranging from 1,500 to an incredible 12,000.

When sanding larger areas a Grip-a-Disc system is useful. A special rubber pad with a Velcro surface is fitted in the chuck of a small electric drill and 50mm diameter discs of abrasive paper are attached.

Points to remember when sanding:

Power sanding a flat surface, using a drill holding a Grip-a-Disc. The blank is sycamore and the decorative circle in the centre is snakewood.

Sanding a twelfth-scale birdbath turned from sycamore on the Unimat. The toolrest has been removed.

- move the toolrest right out of the way;
- hold the abrasive beneath the revolving spindle work;
- keep the abrasive moving to reduce the risk of building up sanding lines;
- work up through the grits;
- avoid over-sanding, especially on very small spindles, in order to retain the crisp detail.

BURNISHING

A non-woven web abrasive is extremely useful for burnishing the wood after sanding. This type of abrasive, which resembles a pan scourer, consists of a mesh of nylon fibres on to which aluminium oxide or silicon carbide grains are firmly bonded by resin. As the grain is used up, fresh grain becomes exposed.

Giving a boxwood nutcracker a final burnish with a handful of boxwood shavings held under the work.

The mesh is non-clogging and it can be washed out and reused many times. It is superior to wire wool, which is hard on the hands, rusts and often leaves traces of metal filings behind.

As well as burnishing, the web abrasive is also good for applying polish and for de-nibbing between coats of paint. A piece may also be burnished by holding a handful of shavings under the rotating wood.

SEALING

Cellulose sanding sealer can be applied with a cloth to bare wood on a stationary lathe. Gently rotate the wood by hand and de-nibb before applying a second coat. Cellulose-based products give off very strong fumes and should only be used in a well-ventilated area and when wearing a mask. This product fills the grain and gives a durable base for further polishing.

POLISHING

To bring up the beauty of the grain, and to protect the wood from dirt and grease, it is advisable to polish finished pieces. This can be done in a number of ways.

Finishing Oils

These oils are easy to apply to bare, sanded wood and are particularly suitable for toys and items for the kitchen because they are non-toxic. They are practically odourless, free of unpleasant solvents, and economical. Apply the oil with a brush and wipe off any surplus after 5 minutes. Allow to dry according to the manufacturer's instructions before applying the next coat. Several coats will give a lustre to the natural wood, and a freshening-up coat can be applied at any time in the future if desired.

Friction Polish

This type of polish is designed to be applied to the rotating wood. It is easy to put on, using soft kitchen paper, and it dries quickly to leave a high gloss shine. At least two coats should be applied, either over cellulose sanding sealer or directly on to bare wood. Friction polish is popular with woodturners because it gives quick results and the beauty of the grain is suddenly revealed as the polish brings the wood to life.

Carnauba Wax

This type of wax is usually sold in stick form and is applied to the rotating wood.

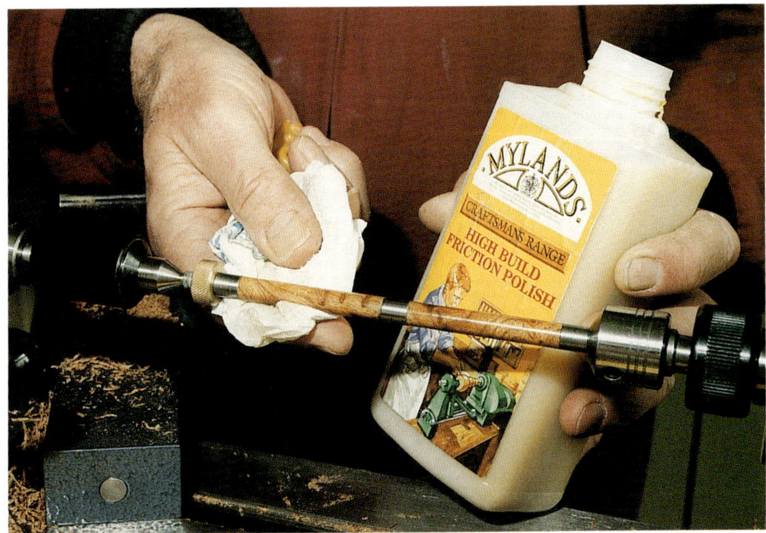

Friction polish being applied to pen barrels turned in burr elm. Several coats will bring up a high shine. It is easy to apply and the results are instant.

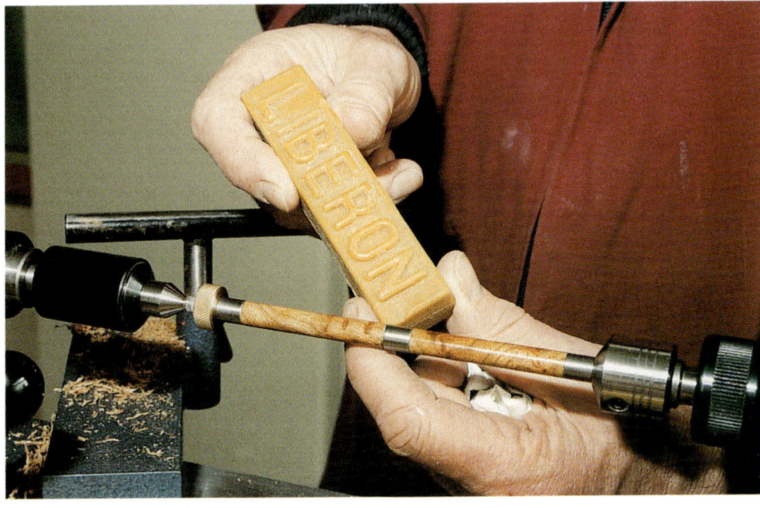

Applying a final coat of wax on top of the friction polish.

It can be used on top of friction polish, over cellulose sealer or directly on to bare wood. Rub the stick over the rotating piece and, using a cloth or tissue, move the hand backwards and forwards under the wood until a high gloss is achieved. Wax is non-toxic and pleasant to use, with hardly any smell.

BUFFING

A final buffing up on a polishing wheel is particularly effective with close-grain woods such as boxwood and for removing any tiny scratches on artificial materials. Calico polishing mops can be held in the lathe on a taper screw type arbor, often referred to as a 'pigtail'. The arbor has a parallel shank that can be held in the jaws of a chuck. Pigtails can also be fitted direct to a bench grinder in place of the stone.

Two types of polishing mop produce the best possible finish on fine-grain woods and alternative materials. The first type is a loose-leaf, or open mop consisting of up to fifty thin discs of white

Buffing up a little box turned in boxwood with a inlay of artificial mother-of-pearl. The polishing is carried out using T-cut (red can) and a close-stitched mop mounted on the wheel of a grinder.

material held together in the centre by two leather washers, with a centre hole for an arbor or tapered spigot. The second type is closely stitched, with the stitching spiralling out from the centre to the outer circumference. This mop also has leather washers and a hole for an arbor. The stitched mop is stiffer than the loose-leaf type and is used for more aggressive polishing whereas the loose-leaf mop flows over gentle curves giving an even polishing action. The buffing is carried out by applying fine wax polish to the wood, and holding the piece against the edge of the rotating mop, constantly turning it to obtain an even finish.

Always wear eye protection or, better still, a full-face visor when using a polishing mop, even if you wear glasses. Threads from the mop, mixed with the polishing compound, may bombard the skin and cause irritation. If the polishing mop is used in the lathe, work from the other side of the machine so that particles are directed away from you.

STAINING AND COLOURING

Many woodturners prefer to leave wood in its natural state, but sometimes it will need to be stained to represent other woods, when producing model furniture, for example. Toys are usually more appealing to children if they are brightly painted.

With all finishing products, stains and paints, take the trouble to read the manufacturer's instructions before starting work. Experiment beforehand on scrap pieces similar to the wood used for the main work. This is particularly important when staining wood to make sure that the desired colour will be achieved.

Staining

There are many exciting acrylic-based wood stains and dyes. Some represent woods and are particularly useful for modelling – for example, pearwood can be stained to look like mahogany – while others are pastel or bright colours. These stains must be applied to bare wood before any polishing is done.

Painting

There are many acrylic craft paints available, in a huge array of colours. They are inexpensive and easy to use, and dry very quickly. One added bonus is that the brushes used will wash out easily in water. Because they are water-based, acrylic paints do tend to raise the wood grain and it is wise to de-nibb between coats.

Paint with the wood still held on the lathe whenever possible. Apply a base priming coat and, when this is dry, sand right back to the wood using non-woven web abrasive. Repeat the process to achieve a really smooth surface for painting.

Varnishing

When painting or staining is complete, a matt, silk or gloss acrylic varnish can be

Applying a pastel peppermint wood dye to a small bud vase.

brushed or sprayed on. Always check first with some paint or stain on scrap wood to be absolutely sure that the varnish will not cause colours to weep. Spirit markers can work well, but the varnish occasionally acts as a solvent, with disastrous results.

> A poor finish can ruin a piece of work, however well it is turned.

— 6 —

PLANNING AND PREPARATION

It is worth taking the trouble to plan a project before commencing work. Indeed, the process of sitting down with an A4 drawing board and a pencil to work out how an item is going to be turned, and arriving at a pleasing shape and design, can be very enjoyable. In scale modelling it is vital to get the proportions and measurements right. Even an artistic piece of work will benefit from sketches of possible shapes and ideas being made before the blank is put on the lathe.

For repeat items, say, a number of identical spindles, it is always beneficial to make a turning guide (*see* the example below) and a template from the drawing. The template is used to check the actual shape of the piece as turning progresses.

A drawing was made for the largest candlestick, which is 100mm high. The drawing was then reduced on a photocopier for the 50mm candlestick and again for the smallest, 25mm high. The candlesticks were turned in boxwood together with the candles, which were then painted.

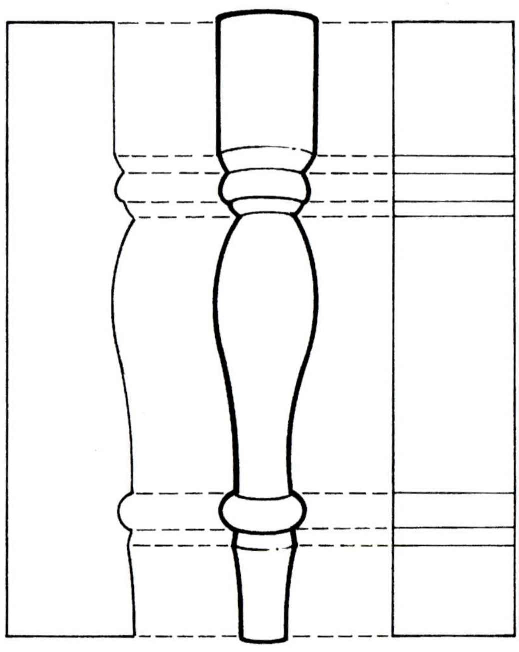

Turning guide and template for a table leg.

Turning guide for a finial. The main datum lines are transferred to the cylinder in pencil.

Cutting out a template for a knob with a powered fretsaw.

PREPARATION

The following steps are involved before turning can even start:

1. Bring the wood to be used into the workshop to settle.
2. Do research if necessary.
3. Make sketches and take measurements if possible.
4. Draw a plan to scale; if the item is very small, scale up the drawing so that you can see what you are doing.
5. Make a turning guide.
6. Make a template.
7. Decide how the wood blank is going to be held on the lathe with the equipment at your disposal.
8. Prepare the wood to go on the lathe.

Everything is now set for turning to begin.

MEASURING

Being able to measure accurately is important, especially when making models to scale. The measurements required are lengths and widths, diameters, thicknesses of material and depths of holes. The following equipment will be needed for measuring; some of these instruments will also be needed at the planning stage.

STAINLESS STEEL RULER

A 300mm ruler calibrated in metric and imperial is essential. Modellers who work in 1⁄12in scale for dolls'-house furniture and fittings will find it a considerable advantage to have a ruler calibrated in twelfths; most dolls' house specialists can supply these. Wooden rulers can be marked out to suit other scales.

The lathe should be stopped before taking measurements with Vernier callipers or micrometers, to avoid damage to the work, the instrument or to the turner.

SMALL SQUARE

A small square is used for marking out wood and for checking squareness and flatness.

SPRING-BOW COMPASS OR DIVIDERS

These instruments are used for drawing out circles and arcs and for comparative measuring. The dividers are also useful for taking off measurements from a drawing.

PROPORTIONAL DIVIDERS

These dividers are designed for scaling up and down and are calibrated and set so that dimensions can be increased or decreased accurately when rescaling a drawing.

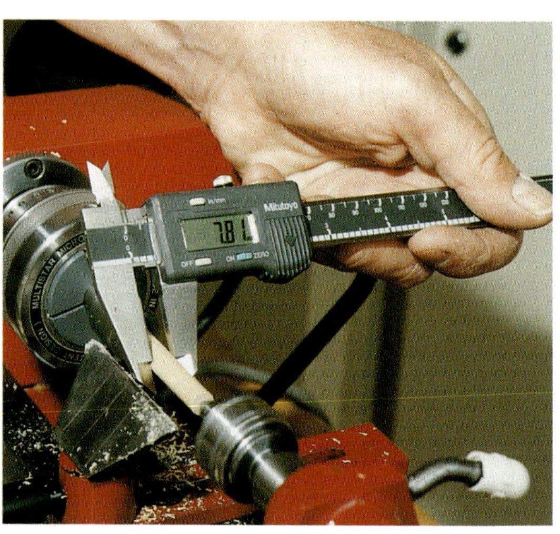

Digital callipers are very easy to read, but they are expensive.

VERNIER CALLIPER

The Vernier calliper is undoubtedly the most useful measuring tool for miniature work. Some turners may find the conventional scale difficult to read and a calliper with a dial on it is much simpler to use. The digital callipers with their instant read-out in metric or imperial are the easiest of all to use but they are also the most expensive.

Dial gauge callipers used to take off a measurement from a drawing.

Callipers are available in hardened stainless steel or in reinforced nylon, which has several advantages. It will not rust and will not damage the surface of the wood being measured. Because nylon callipers are lighter there is also less likelihood of breaking very thin spindles. However, if the callipers are used on rotating wood – bad practice, but often done – the friction will cause damage to the nylon.

Some digital callipers will read to 0.1 of a millimetre, while the more expensive are even more precise, reading to 0.01 of a millimetre.

Very cheap steel or plastic callipers are best avoided.

DEPTH GAUGE

A dedicated depth gauge is used particularly for box making and to check depth when carrying out hollowing-out work. Sometimes it is useful to make a one-off gauge from wood as an aid to repetitive work.

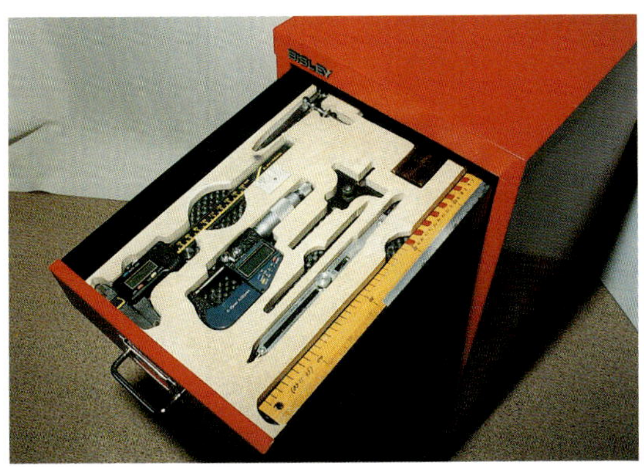

Measuring instruments need to be carefully stored.

THE MICROMETER

This instrument will not be needed by all woodturners but it is very useful for accurate, small-diameter work, for example, when making pens or lace bobbins. It is an excellent aid for checking spigot diameters turned for collet chucks. Affordable digital micrometers are much easier to read and increasingly available.

> If you plan your work, success is guaranteed – if you do not, failure is inevitable!

— 7 —

DRILLING, INDEXING AND THREAD CUTTING

DRILLING

Woodturners frequently need to drill holes in a blank. These might be pilot holes, used to mount wood on a screwchuck or to attach a blank to a faceplate; a number of equally spaced holes purely for decoration; or, in the case of a model or a toy, a series of spaced holes around a hub, to take the spokes of a wheel.

Drilling can be done either on or off the lathe. There are many ways of carrying out drilling holes accurately and there are examples throughout this book. Modellers may already have some of the equipment mentioned.

EQUIPMENT

Electric Drill

There are a number of small mains, cordless, or 12v DC power drills to choose from. A mains drill usually gives better value for money, but a cordless drill will come in handy too. As well as being used for straightforward drilling, the power tool can also hold sanding discs and burrs when shaping and carrying out decorative work.

Drills of very small diameter are less likely to be broken using a small, precision electric drill than with a manual hand drill.

Greater accuracy can be achieved with the drill fitted in a stand. When selecting a

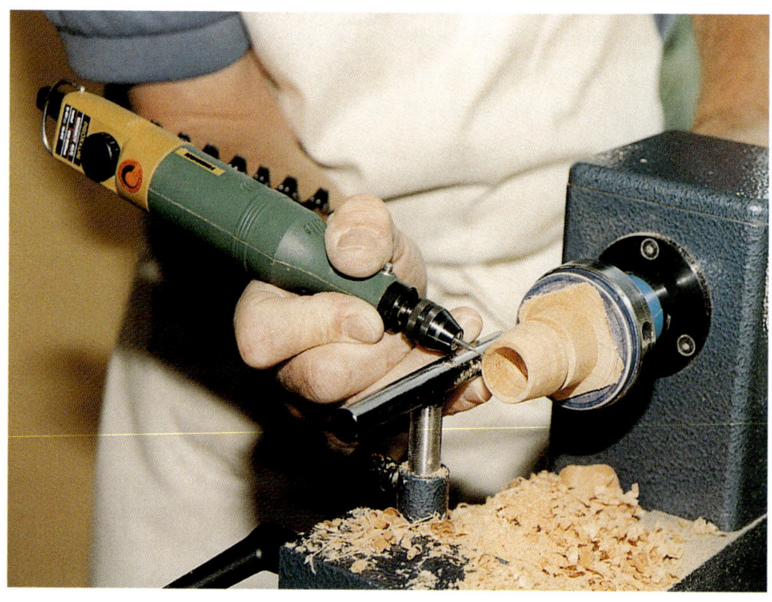

The Proxxon Micromot 40 drill is a useful small drill for free-hand drilling.

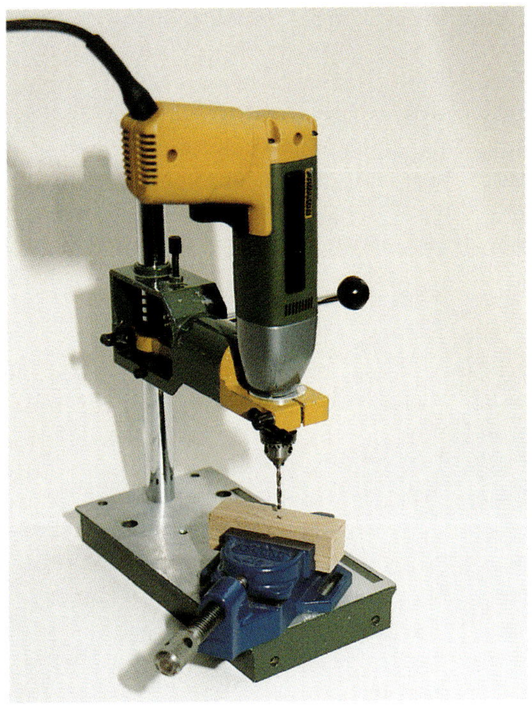

The Proxxon Colt 100w mains drill fitted in a Proxxon Micromot MBS140 drillstand provides the equivalent of a small bench drill. The distance between the column to the centre of the drill is 140mm and the vertical travel is 30mm. The stand has a built-in depth stop. The Colt has a 6mm Jacob's-type chuck and the electronic variable speed is controlled by means of a trigger, giving speeds from 0 to 3,000rpm.

Two very fine holes being drilled close together in one end of a spindle. The Proxxon compound table is calibrated to 0.05mm. The travel on the X axis is 134mm and on the Y axis 46mm. With the machine vice mounted on the compound table, the turner has complete control.

drillstand, remember that the collar diameter on small drills is not standard.

Vice

A small machine vice, which will hold round or square stock, is essential to hold work firmly and safely on the table during the drilling operation.

Bench Drill

A small bench drill will prove to be invaluable for the accurate drilling of many holes. A dedicated bench drill tends to be more precise than a drill held in a drillstand because there is less likelihood of any movement or play. When it is combined with a compound table and machine vice, the workshop has an excellent system.

The drillstand, or even the pillar drill, can be adapted for use on the lathe itself. Turn up a pillar in hardwood, or commission a local engineering firm to turn one up in steel, designed to fit into the toolrest holder, so that a drill can be positioned over the work in the lathe.

Flexible Drive

A flexible drive can be run off the lathe or from a power drill or bench drill. The shaft needs to be very flexible but robust enough to avoid any kinking when placed under load. A flexible drive is useful for freehand drilling and for sanding and shaping with burrs. A small keyless chuck or a collet chuck is usually fitted.

The grooves in this finial are being formed with a burr held in a collet chuck at the end of a flexible drive. The positions for the grooves were marked first, using the indexing facility on the chuck.

Collet Chucks

Many small drills are fitted with collet chucks as standard, with a number of collets designed to take accessories of a specific diameter. A good collet chuck is accurate and fairly small in diameter, but a number of collets in various sizes will be needed. Because the collets are so small they can be easily lost in shavings.

Keyed or Keyless Chucks?

The better-quality small chucks are operated by means of a key and are designed like a traditional Jacob's-type chuck. The keyless chuck is usually finger-tightened, although tommy bars or spanners are often also provided. Although these chucks are easier to use, and more versatile, some still prefer the keyed chuck, which does hold the accessory very firmly.

Hand Pin Chucks

Sometimes, a manual hole may need to be made in the centre of the end of a turned item, for example, when turning a small vase. A pin chuck with a fine twist drill fitted is an ideal way of producing such a hole, which may be opened out during turning. Pin chucks with collets, or finger-tightened chucks, are produced by a number of manufacturers; simply turn up a wooden handle for the one you choose.

Twist Drills

There is a huge range of HSS twist drills in all conceivable sizes. For the very smallest work it is possible to purchase drills with standard 2.35mm shanks but with drilling ends from 2mm down to 0.6mm. This means that they can be used in a standard collet. It is very easy to break small drills and as they are relatively expensive items for their size this design has an advantage. Centre drills are designed with spiral flutes to give a long life. They have a small-diameter starting drill with a wider-diameter body and are ideal when accurate drilling is needed.

Small-sized drills can be found in specialist catalogues catering for model engineers and watchmakers.

It is important that the work to be drilled is held firmly in a vice, or cramped to a table, because small drills are easily broken. Do not be tempted to hold the work by hand; if the drill slips the results can be very painful.

DRILLING TECHNIQUES

On the Lathe Between Centres

Often it is convenient to drill a centre hole in a blank held on the headstock. To do this you will need a 6 or 8mm capacity Jacob's-type drill chuck threaded at the back ⅜ × 24tpi so that a MT shank can be fitted. The drill chuck can then be held in the tailstock.

First, check that your headstock and tailstock line up accurately – this is essential when centre drilling. With the lathe running, advance the drill slowly into the revolving work. Withdraw every so often to allow the shavings to clear, otherwise the drill bit could overheat and jam. To drill to a certain depth, make a temporary depth stop by wrapping a piece of coloured tape around the twist drill.

From the Side or From the Front

A proprietary drilling jig consists of a stem that fits into the toolrest holder and a top that takes collets drilled through horizontally to guide specified drill diameters accurately. The object of the exercise is to ensure that the twist drill stays horizontal and does not wander. The drill guides are usually machined to take drills from 3mm diameter upwards; for drills under 3mm, another method needs to be used.

The wood to be drilled is held in the headstock and the lathe is stationary. This is one occasion when a cordless drill comes into its own, with no mains cable to get in the way.

When equally spaced holes are needed – around the hub of a wheel, for example – it is essential for the holes to be drilled with the correct distance between them. Doing this manually in small scale is quite difficult and built-in indexing in the lathe, or on the chuck body, is therefore a great advantage.

INDEXING

Being able to index turned items in the lathe is very useful when drilling holes that need to be accurately positioned, when marking precise positions and for decorative work. Most lathes, and many chucks, are indexed with twenty-four equally spaced holes, giving a choice of two, three, four, six, eight, twelve and twenty-four divisions. The picture on page 65 shows the combination of divisions that can be achieved. A pin, or an arm with a pin, is used to lock the spindle or chuck in the selected hole. Great care must be taken to ensure that the lathe is not started with the pin in position.

Some numbers of divisions, for example, ten, will need to be marked out manually (*see* the picture on page 65). Builders of model ships will often find that the number of divisions they require cannot be achieved with standard indexing, and they will need to mark out the number of divisions using the DIY method.

THREAD CUTTING

Joining can be done by turning spigots, drilling holes and glueing pieces together, but cutting screws and threads is an added challenge to the turner and it is fun to do. Thread cutting was the method of joining used in the past both to avoid any wastage

The index bar pin is used to lock the chuck so that it does not move while free-hand drilling takes place with a very fine twist drill in a flexible drive. The thumb holds the bar in the chuck firmly and the toolrest is used as a guide.

A number of holes being drilled around the side of a wheel hub with the aid of a Sorby drilling jig. The lathe is stationary and locked in position.

Four equally spaced holes being drilled using the Multistar Bore-Mate on the face of a partly turned blank. A home-made depth stop has been fabricated from a plastic tube and a washer. The lathe is stationary and locked in position.

The positions for the engine cylinders on this toy aeroplane were marked out and drilled using indexing and a drill jig. The propeller was first turned as a disc and then divided into three using indexing.

If two discs are joined by spindles, as on this egg timer, the holes must be exactly aligned. Indexing and drilling on the lathe will ensure accuracy.

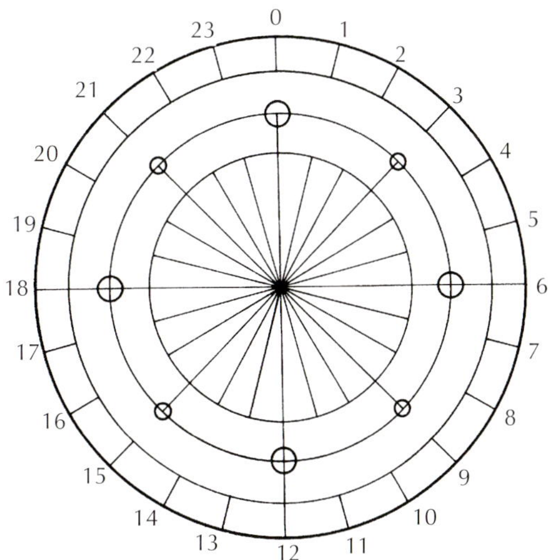

Indexing with twenty-four holes.

The Selbix Mini has built-in indexing. The pin, shown on a key ring, is pushed in to lock the spindle in the selected hole. It is both simple to use and effective. One hole has been painted to show the starting point.

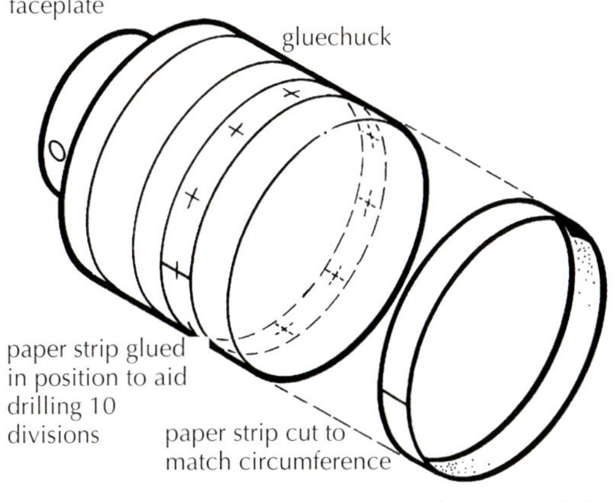

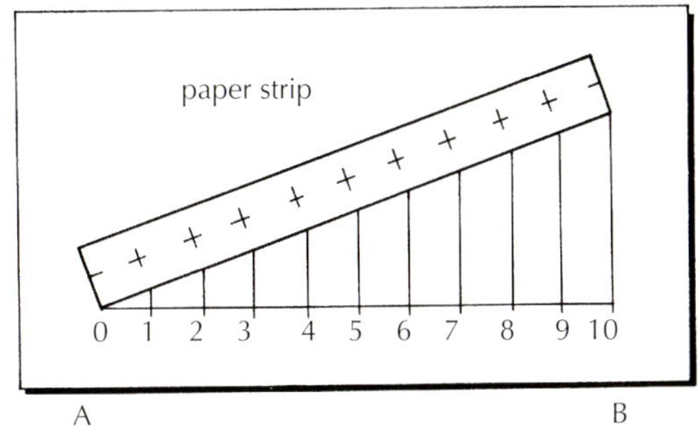

DIY dividing.

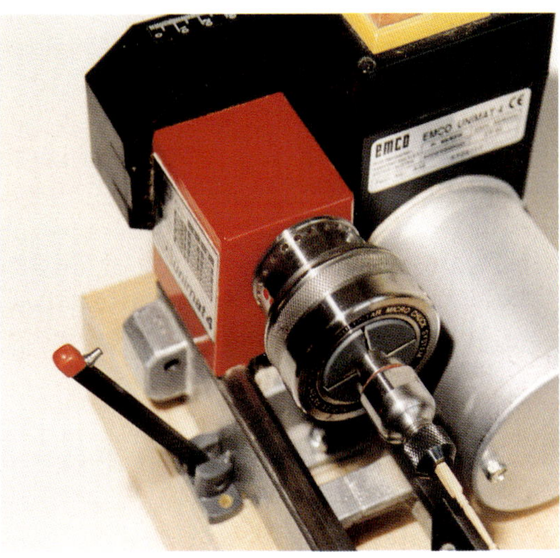

The Multistar Micro chuck is indexed and an arm with a pin locks the lathe in position.

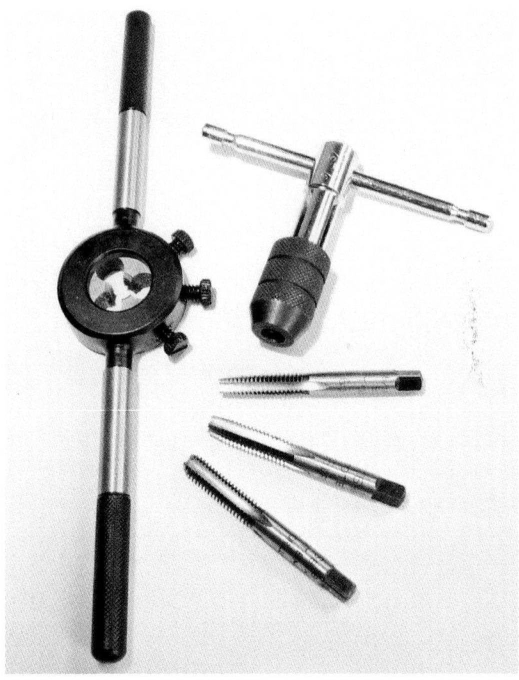

5⁄16W taps, tapholder die and die holder.

of precious material, such as ivory, and also to make any subsequent renovation or repair easier to carry out. An ivory chess man joined in this way, for example, may be restored by unscrewing the pieces and replacing only the part that is damaged. This type of joint should not be glued together otherwise future restoration will be difficult.

There are three main methods of thread cutting:

- using taps and dies
- hand chasing
- using a screwbox

USING TAPS AND DIES

Taps and dies can be used very effectively to cut a thread in such materials as cast polyester resin. Threads can also be cut in very fine-grained hardwoods such as boxwood, but the results are not as crisp.

Because there are so many different types and sizes of threads it is wise to standardize on a few sizes and keep the taps, dies and tapping drills together to avoid wasting time searching for the correct sizes. A practical starting size for miniature work is 5⁄16inW. (Whitworth threads are always expressed in imperial measurement.) A 5⁄16W tap and die will produce a thread with 18 teeth per inch and an outside diameter of 5⁄16in.

Woodturners who turn fine-grain woods, ivory, bone and artificial materials, and enjoy precision work, may wish to consider purchasing a die holder, which can be held in the tailstock of the lathe. A tailstock die holder will hold a split die so that a thread can be cut on the end of a spindle held in a chuck in the headstock with absolute accuracy. The work is rotated by hand – woodturning lathes will not rotate at the very low speeds that are possible with a metal-turning lathe. The die holder will hold four outside sizes of dies and can be set accurately to compensate for any possible misalignment between headstock and tailstock. Die holders, which are expensive, are available from model engineering suppliers.

Drilling a Tapping Hole

The first stage is to drill a tapping hole with an HSS twist drill. Mechanical tables give the correct tapping size drill for the numerous sizes and types of thread. For 5⁄16W threads, a tapping drill of 6.5mm diameter will be required. Experiment first on a scrap of the material you are going to use to ensure that your tapping hole is the right size.

Cutting with a Tap

A tap is used for cutting internal threads. The tap is a hardened steel bolt, ground to give cutting edges to form a screw pattern in a pre-drilled hole. Taps are made in sets of three: a *taper*, a *second* and a *plug*. The taper tap has its leading end tapered off for eight to ten threads, the second is less tapered with only two to three threads chamfered and the plug has no tapering at all. For a 'through hole' the second is all that is needed but for 'blind holes' – with one end only open – all three taps need to be used.

Cutting a Thread Through a Thin Piece of Material

First drill a tapping hole with the drill fitted in a pillar drill. Use some scrap backing behind the piece to be drilled, to avoid any tearing as the drill breaks through. Hold the second tap in a tap holder and rotate into the hole to cut the thread. Once the tap starts to cut, stop and reverse out to allow the shavings to clear, otherwise the newly cut thread could be stripped. Take your time, be gentle and keep the tap at right-angles to the work.

Cutting a Thread in a Blind Hole

Drill the tapping hole two or three threads deeper than the finished depth required. Hold the taper tap in a tap holder and begin to cut the thread, withdrawing from time to time to clear the swarf. Be careful not to force the tap when the end comes into contact with the bottom of the hole. Repeat the process with the second tap and then finish off with the plug tap.

Cutting an External Thread on a Spigot Using a Split Die

This type of die has a split, which permits a small amount of adjustment in the diameter of thread the die will cut by springing it a small amount open or closed by means of three screws in the die holder. When buying a die, make sure that you have a die holder to match its outside diameter, because these do vary. Turn an accurate spigot 7mm diameter for a 5⁄16W thread. Cut the thread by rotating the die on to the spigot by hand, withdrawing

Earring stand turned from artificial ivory and screwed together in two places with 5⁄16W threaded spigots, produced with a standard tap and die. The top disc and base are turned from sheet material and the knob and pillar from rod.

every so often to remove the shavings. Continue until the face of the die comes into contact with the shoulder of the spigot. Remove the die. Use a Swiss file to relieve the area between the shoulder and the extent to which the thread is cut. This is done to ensure that the spindle will thread right up to the shoulder, to give a flush fit. If the area close to the shoulder is turned prior to cutting the thread, there is a chance that the cast polyester will break as the thread is cut.

HAND CHASING

Hand chasing is the traditional method used by boxwood and ivory turners for striking threads and produces good results in close-grained woods and in cast polyester resin. The main advantage of this method is that it allows threads to be cut to any diameter, making it particularly useful for boxes with screwed lids.

Using chasers is an acquired skill and needs a good deal of practice. The tools are usually made from carbon steel and are in effect form tools. They are designed to cut internal and external threads on work rotating on the lathe at slow speed.

Cutting an internal thread on a turned box with a chaser. The Sorby chaser has 16tpi.

A dice shaker with a compartment for the dice. The two halves are screwed together with a chased thread.

Start with a pair of chasers ground to cut threads of 18tpi. This ties up with the 5⁄16W size, which also cuts threads of 18tpi. The tools usually come with excellent instructions and there are also videos on the subject. With practice, and a light touch, it is possible to achieve reasonable external and internal threads fairly quickly.

Two chasers are needed in each case – one for the internal thread and one for the external.

USING A SCREWBOX

Screwboxes are used to cut ½, ¾, 1 and 1½in threads (at present only available in imperial sizes) on prepared wooden spindles and a separate one is needed for each size. The ½in is probably the most useful for this scale of turning. The wooden box has handles and inside there is a V-shaped cutter and a screw guide. When rotated on the spindle, the box cuts a thread in the same manner as a large die.

This type of thread is used for flower presses, nutcrackers, tapestry frames and

A ½in screwbox with a turned and threaded spigot.

These three nutcrackers are all turned in boxwood. The central screw, which is activated by turning the top knob, is produced with a ½in screwbox and the corresponding thread in the body is cut with a matching ½in tap.

similar items. On a hardwood, the thread cut is usually crisp but the results on softwoods can be disappointing. A matching tap is provided with the set for internal thread cutting and a plug tap is available as an extra to use for cutting blind holes.

Producing an accurate thread is very satisfying.

— 8 —

USEFUL TECHNIQUES

GLUE CHUCKING

This technique is used frequently in miniature turning, because it is quick and easy to set up. Afterwards, clean off any glue residue and skim off the surface of the glue chuck if necessary, so that the chuck can be used many times. It is an advantage to have a spare faceplate with a glue chuck permanently fitted.

A glue chuck is made as follows:

1. To produce a glue chuck suitable for a 50mm faceplate, cut a blank 55mm diameter from 30mm thicknessed hardwood roughly to the round.
2. Drill 6 × 2mm diameter pilot holes in the blank and screw it to the faceplate with 25mm long, No 6 countersunk wood screws.
3. Turn the blank to the round to match the diameter of the faceplate and face off the end so that it is absolutely flat; check with a straight edge.
4. Cut shallow rings on the face of the glue chuck. This is useful when centring small pieces of wood and it also improves adhesion.
5. Turn a shallow V cut on the outside of the blank to indicate where the ends of the woodscrews come.
6. Mark the edge of the glue chuck, and file a permanent register mark on the edge of the faceplate, so that the two marks can be accurately lined up again after removal and remounting of the glue chuck.

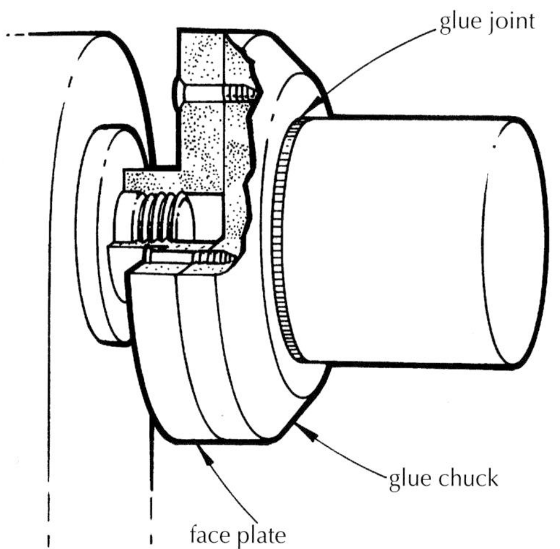

Glue chucking.

ADHESIVES FOR GLUE CHUCKING

Hot-Melt Glue

This type of adhesive is particularly suitable for glue chucking. Three blobs of 60-second high-tack glue will hold a blank very firmly to a glue chuck, and 60 seconds is long enough time to locate the blank accurately on the glue chuck. Beware, hot-melt glue is extremely hot when it leaves the gun and can burn the skin, but it cools and sets very rapidly. Once the glue gun has been purchased, the 295mm-long sticks are relatively inexpensive. Work can be prised off the chuck with a knife and any remaining glue residue is easily scraped off.

Superglue

These fast-action adhesives work well but they are expensive, particularly when used with an activator, and many have a limited

Applying hot-melt-glue with a Bosch glue gun to a blank ready to put on the glue chuck (coloured red). Hot liquid glue is dispensed when the gun trigger is pulled. The glue stick has a diameter of 11mm and started life 295mm long. The white dot on the chuck lines up with the arrow on the faceplate and the line round the circumference shows the position of the ends of the screws inserted through the back of the faceplate.

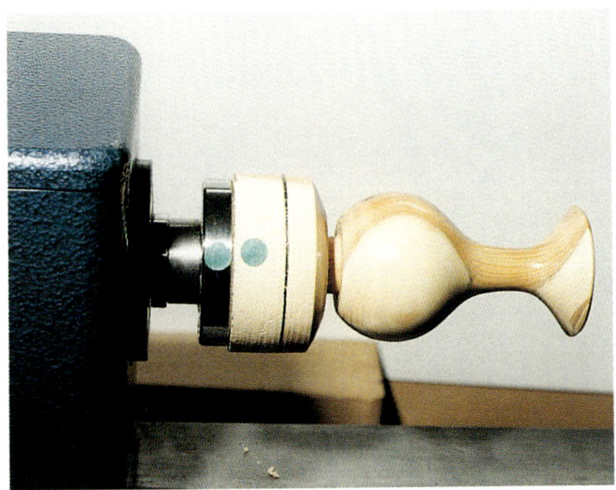

Completed yew vase about to be parted off, after turning on a glue chuck held on a faceplate. The two green dots allow the chuck to be remounted if necessary so that the work will run true. The outer edge of the glue chuck has been chamfered to produce a smooth edge and to give easier access to the bottom of the vase.

shelf life. They are extensively used by woodturners and provide an instant, very strong, bond.

PVA

General-purpose woodworking adhesive is more than adequate but more patience and planning is required because the blank needs to be cramped to the chuck and the glue left to cure.

Contact Adhesive

A solvent-free contact adhesive, such as Copydex, is very good for holding thin discs on a glue chuck. The adhesive is applied to the back of the wood blank and the blank is then pressed firmly to the glue chuck. When turning plastic material, a thin coat is applied to the back of the blank and to the face of the glue chuck; after 20 minutes the two surfaces can be pressed firmly together. The item can be prised off the glue chuck with a knife once turning is complete and any remaining glue can easily be cleaned off.

Carpet Tape

Thin discs and lightweight blanks can be temporarily stuck to the glue chuck with heavy-duty double-sided carpet tape. Cramping up the mounted work and leaving it under pressure for 15 minutes dramatically improves the strength of the bond. Blanks glued to the chuck in this way can be turned to produce small platters and discs. When turning blanks held in this way, use tailstock support wherever practical.

JAM CHUCKING

A jam chuck is a temporary wooden chuck designed to hold partly turned work, so that the reverse side can be turned, sanded and polished. Turn a spigot on the

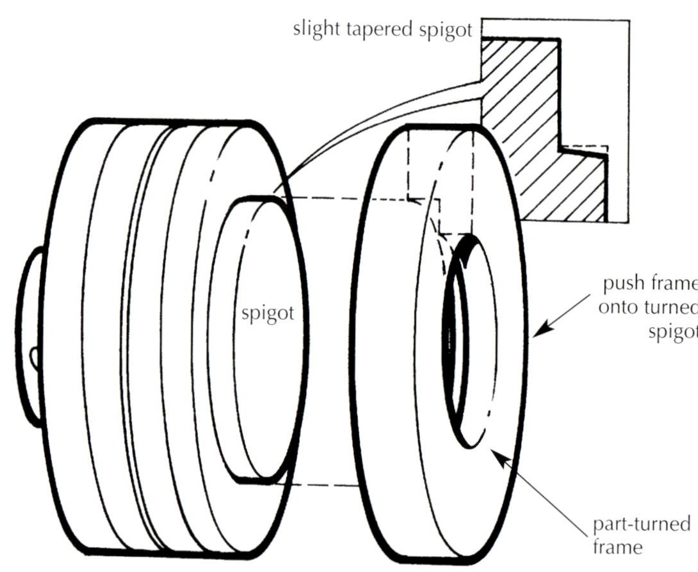

Jam chucking.

The wood on the glue chuck has been turned to form a jam chuck and the partly turned work is about to be pushed on so that the front surface of the frame can be turned.

remaining wood held on the chuck with a diameter to match the internal diameter of the item to be held. Take care, to ensure a good snug fit – if it is too tight, it can crack the wood; turning the spigot slightly tapered from the front to the back is also good practice. The work to be finished is then pushed on.

This technique is used in Exercises 3 and 9 (*see* Chapter 10, pages 91 and 106), in turning a frame and a box.

USING THE SCREWCHUCK

A prepared and drilled blank about to be screwed on to a Peter Child screwchuck. The disc of plywood (painted red) protects the face of the chuck from damage by the turning tool.

The screwchuck is easy to use, requiring only one central hole drilled to a depth that equals the length of the screw. A simple depth stop on the drill will ensure that the pilot hole is always drilled to the correct depth. The diameter of the pilot hole will depend upon the diameter of the chuck screw. When turning softwood, the pilot hole can be slightly smaller than when turning hardwood; it is worth experimenting to find the correct size for a satisfactory grip. Save time searching for equipment by storing the appropriate drills with the chuck.

The screwchuck is most commonly used for holding a bowl or platter blank so that the outside shape can be turned. After the shaping has been done, a dovetail spigot, or a recess, is turned on the base and the partly turned bowl is transferred to a combination chuck. The inside is then turned and the bowl is completed.

This very small yew bowl was turned in one operation on a screwchuck. Although this may seem wasteful on wood, it can be done without a combination chuck. The material left on the screwchuck can be used as a glue chuck.

PRESSURE CHUCKING

This is a good method for holding thin discs of plywood or thicknessed hardwood, allowing them to be turned to produce small table tops or backs for frames, for example.

Prepare the equipment as follows:

1. Make two pads from 30mm thicknessed hardwood. Mark out 2 × 55mm diameter circles and cut them roughly to the round. Screw the first one to a faceplate and turn it to a diameter of 50mm. Glue some rubber to the surface.
2. Take the second blank and centre pop on one side. Countersink the centre pop to match the point of a revolving centre. Position the second blank so that it is contact with the rubber face of the first blank and bring up the tailstock to hold it firmly in position. Turn the second blank to 50mm, to match the first.
3. Release the tailstock pressure and glue rubber to the un-popped surface.

To use the pressure pad method, roughly cut the thicknessed disc you wish to turn and place it between the two pressure pads, bringing up the tailstock fitted with a revolving centre to provide axial pressure. Turn the rim of the disc to the round and mould the edge, if required.

After the work is removed there will be no marks to indicate how the wood was held.

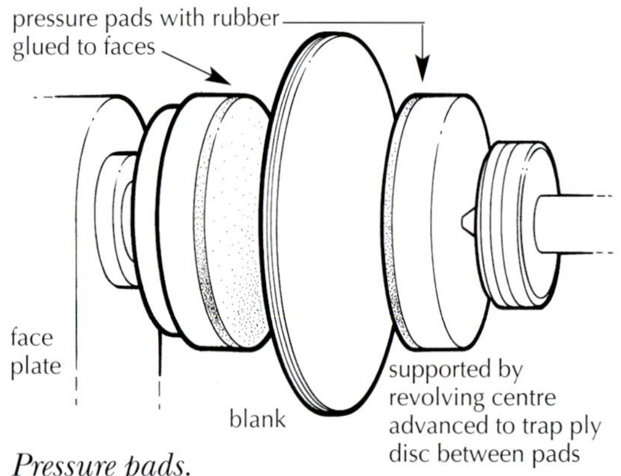

Pressure pads.

SPLIT TURNING

Sometimes a spindle or finial is split down the centre to produce two half turnings; this is known as split turning. To achieve this, two identical blanks are prepared and sandwiched together with PVA glue and a sheet of paper between them. The sandwich is cramped up with two end caps of plywood. Once the glue has cured, the blank can be turned in the normal way. The end caps stop the centres pushing the glued joint apart. The finished work can be gently separated with a penknife to produce two identical halves.

Using the same technique, it is also possible to sandwich four blanks to form quadrants.

With tailstock support the disc is firmly held between the pressure pads so that the edge can be turned and shaped.

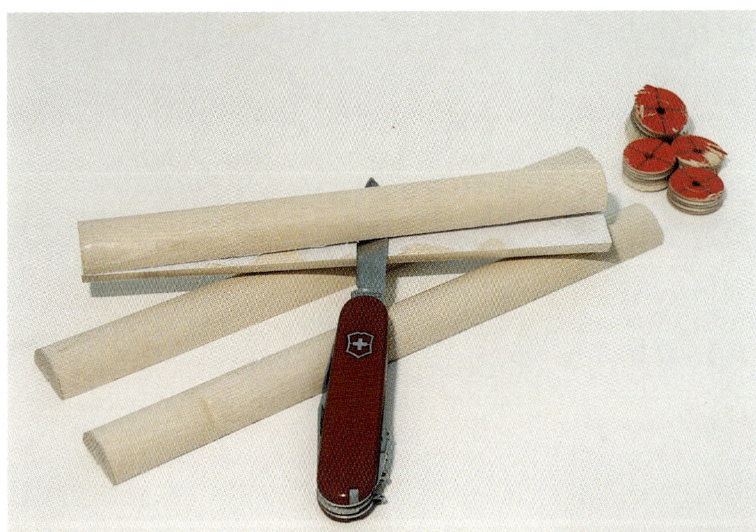

Separating the two halves of a spindle after turning is complete with a penknife. The paper is clearly visible and the remains of the scrap end pieces.

HOLLOWING OUT

A hollowing-out technique may be required when making items such as vases, Christmas finial decorations, or elements for a cot mobile as shown in the photograph. In order to reduce the weight of the balloon for the mobile, a hollowing-out tool was used, to remove as much wood as possible.

Small hollowing-out tools are usually sold in sets of three: one straight tool to start the initial hole, one with a slight hook end to enlarge the hole and the third with a more pronounced hook to finish off the hollowing. These tools are in fact scrapers.

When the tool is out of sight, inside the form, it is easy to forget where the cutting edge is. It should be in a trailing position slightly below the centre line; if it is allowed to come up too far, a dig-in can result. The small entrance hole and inside cavity become choked with shavings very quickly and these are best sucked out with a vacuum. Care must be taken not to go too deep into the form. A piece of coloured tape wrapped round the shank of the tool is useful as a depth gauge, but going through the side occasionally is inevitable.

Small Henry Taylor hollowing-out tool suitable for miniature work. The pencil points to a brass stud, put in to indicate the position of the cutting edge at the end of the hook when it is out of sight inside the hollow form.

There's always a way…

— 9 —

TURNING POLYESTER RESINS

ALTERNATIVE MATERIALS

Books dating from the 1850s, written by Holtzapffel, show ivory and boxwood turning of a very high standard. Today, old pieces are displayed in museums and historic houses, but it is no longer acceptable to use real ivory taken from elephants. Its use now is usually restricted to the restoration work of small items such as cabinet knobs and simple chessmen, using ivory from broken or discarded pieces.

Real ivory has been fashioned by man for many centuries. It is milky cream in colour and can be carved and turned to give fine detail and slender proportions. Although it has a chemical structure similar to bone, it is more dense and homogenous in texture,

A collection of items turned from artificial ivory, bone, tortoiseshell and mother-of-pearl. The synthetic materials work particularly well when inlaid into wooden box lids and knobs.

and less brittle. Today, the animals and the material are protected. Real ivory may not be available for sale, but the synthetic alternatives are so good that they are almost indistinguishable from the original.

Alternative mother-of-pearl can also be purchased. Real mother-of-pearl is a hard, iridescent inner layer that forms in the shells of certain molluscs, such as the pearl oyster. It is composed mainly of calcium carbonate deposited in thin, overlapping layers. The iridescent colours are caused by the interference of reflected light waves. The material is very decorative used as inlay and for making small objects such as jewellery, buttons, knife handles, snuff boxes and fans. Small penknives, for example, often had a mother-of-pearl handle.

Alternative versions of tortoiseshell, abalone, bone, horn and ebony are also available and coloured cast polyester resin material, which comes in both plain and mottled versions, is fun for experiments. A number of other man-made materials (for example, Corian, which is produced for kitchen and bathroom surfaces) turn well; small offcuts are snapped up by turners, particularly pen makers.

Other synthetic materials that can be turned in the woodturning lathe include Perspex, acrylics, ebonite, casein and synthetic pen blanks. Perspex is available from specialist suppliers in a wide variety in conventional and fluorescent colours. Off-cuts of these materials provide the ideal opportunity for experimenting. There are also a number of liquid plastics, which can be either poured into a mould and then turned, or poured directly into turned grooves, to produce a very effective inlay.

ALTERNATIVE IVORY

Synthetic grained ivory is made from cast polyester resin. It looks like, and works like, true ivory and has the grain, general appearance and feel of the real thing. It is non-toxic and has a sweet smell.

Round rods are available in diameters from 15mm up to 120mm diameter in 1.5-metre lengths and the material also comes in disc and sheet form. Rods are probably the most useful sections for turners because they can be chucked with relative ease; however, the sheet material, in thicknesses of 3mm to 3.5mm, is also very useful as an inlay for box lids and for items of jewellery.

This material is expensive but there need be very little wastage; select a diameter as near as possible to the one required, or cut discs from sheet using a powered fretsaw. During turning, long, stringy shavings are formed. They tend to become static and it is advisable to use some form of dust extraction or a workshop vacuum cleaner to deal with this.

TURNING ALTERNATIVE IVORY

Preparation for Glue Chucking

To achieve a true, square end the safest method is to use a mitre saw frame set at a 90-degree angle. For short lengths of rod, first hot-melt-glue the rod to the end of a 35 × 35 × 300mm PAR piece of scrapwood so that the rod can be held firmly by the clamp on the mitre saw frame while cutting.

Safety: never be tempted to cut short lengths of rod on a bandsaw – it is too risky!

Turning Tools

Gouges and skew chisels are not suitable for this form of turning. You will need instead to grind your own tools from HSS blanks, to produce tools with a double symmetrical bevel. *See also* the customized tool in the photograph on page 78. Most tool manufacturers sell unhandled HSS

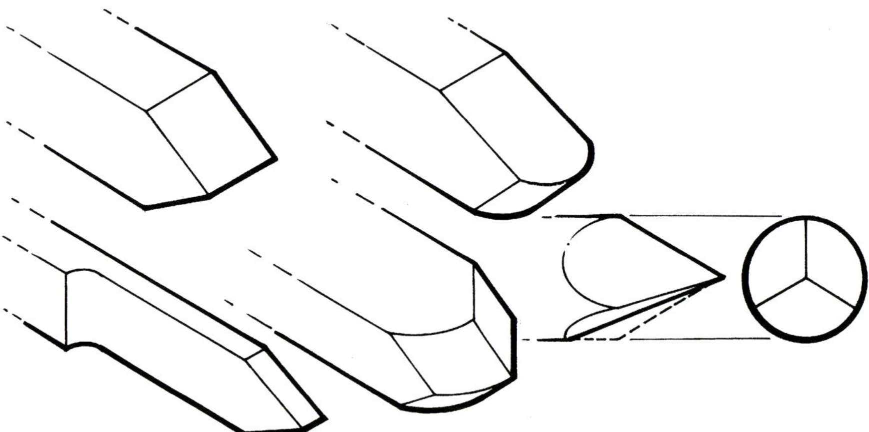

Tools for turning cast polyester resin.

Double-bevel tool designed by Ian Wilkie for turning alternative ivory and boxwood, now produced and sold by Craft Supplies.

blanks, which are usually cheaper at woodworking shows. For some suggested shapes, *see* the picture above.

An armrest will also prove to be invaluable.

Safety: *always* wear eye protection when using the grinder.

Technique

The tools are used with the handle slightly up and with the cutting edge trailing. Position the toolrest so that it is not too close to the work, to allow room to manoeuvre the tool. Set the lathe speed at about 1,500rpm.

This technique takes a little practice at first, since any heavy-handedness results in chips coming off like shrapnel rather than shavings. It is far better to take several gentle cuts than one deep one. Keep tools sharp with regular honing.

Safety: wear a visor for eye and face protection and go gently.

Turning Small Knobs in Alternative Ivory

1. Cut a slice of alternative ivory from a rod a little larger in diameter than the size required for the finished knob.

Large amounts of fine, static shavings are produced when turning cast polyester material but these are not unpleasant and are soon vacuumed away. Although the rod being turned is black (artificial ebony), the shavings are white.

Turning a small blank of cast polyester artificial ivory, mounted on a glue chuck, to produce a knob.

Sand one end absolutely true and glue this to a glue chuck with Superglue or 60-second hot-melt glue. (Glue chucking will lead to the least wastage.)

2. Set the lathe speed to 1,500rpm and begin to shape the top of the knob using a small round-nosed scraper. Use a three-point tool to cut any decorative rings. The shavings cling to the tool and need to be wiped off from time to time, but there is very little dust.
3. Form the waist of the knob with a round-nosed scraper and a parting tool and measure regularly until the right

diameter is achieved. Reduce the speed as the stem gets thinner; the material can become more pliable as it is warmed by friction.

4. Use the finest (1,200-grit) abrasive, although very little sanding should be needed. Apply polish with tissue paper to the rotating knob. Polishes such as T-Cut (red can) or Brasso produce a really high shine and the polish will also remove any scratches or slight imperfections. It is easy to finish a piece of work in the lathe and assume that a perfect finish has been achieved; however, in a better light, and with a magnifying glass (which is recommended), turning marks can often be observed so the polishing operation should not be skimped.
5. With the lathe stationary, cut through the spigot with a fine-toothed saw. This is preferable to parting right through with the turning tool; tiny items have a tendency to fly off the lathe and become lost in the shavings. Very little material will be left on the glue chuck.

INLAID ITEMS

ALTERNATIVE MOTHER-OF-PEARL

Turned box lids are often decorated with inserts of cast polyester mother-of-pearl and alternative ivory. Real mother-of-pearl is an extraordinarily hard material for turning, producing a very fine, dangerous dust. A face mask is vital. Synthetic mother-of-pearl is much easier to turn, with fine shavings, and very little dust. It comes in white or oyster, and a sheet has an uneven, patterned surface. When the top layer is turned away, the iridescent mother-of-pearl effect is produced.

An alternative method of turning very small knobs in artificial ivory. The rod is held in a drill chuck so that two matching knobs can be turned for a small cabinet. The Record drill chuck screws directly on to the headstock spindle so that it cannot work loose during turning.

Cutting Alternative Mother-of-Pearl Sheet Material

To cut the mother-of-pearl into discs ready for turning, a powered fretsaw, set at a fairly slow speed and fitted with a No 7 blade, works very well. If the machine is run at too high a speed, fusing may occur and the blade will stick to the work. The blade must be really sharp and the rate of feed not too great, otherwise there is a risk of chipping at the exit end of the cut. Masking tape on the underside of the sheet reduces this risk.

Cut carefully and economically to minimize wastage, and keep any offcuts, which may come in useful at a later date.

Some of the sheet material has a slightly powdery back, which needs to be removed by rubbing over a flat sanding surface. Double-sided heavy-duty carpet tape can be used effectively for holding the material on to a glue chuck. Cramp the disc to the chuck and leave for 20 minutes. It is important that the glue chuck surface is exactly flat and that it is at least the same diameter as the disc to be turned.

Turning the Discs

Turn the surface with a double-bevelled scraper. The curved cutting edge is used to scrape the surface from the centre line outwards and the tool is rested on the armrest. Take gentle cuts and try to avoid forming a 'pimple' or 'dimple' in the centre. Work in a good light and keep tools really sharp.

Tidy up the edge with a parting tool, making sure that it is absolutely at right-angles. If this is not done well, there will be an unsightly gap between the material and the wood when the insert is finally in place.

Finishing

Sand carefully with ultra-fine abrasive and then polish with T-Cut or Brasso until the

Pressure is applied with soft-jawed cramps to improve adhesion between the cast polyester resin disc and the glue chuck when using double-sided heavy-duty carpet tape.

Wood and synthetic materials can be used effectively together. The body of this figure, and the box on which it stands, is turned in boxwood and the hat, cane, legs and boots are turned in cast polyester resin. The parts are joined together with cast polyester resin rod threaded 5⁄16W and the corresponding holes are tapped to match.

surface is really smooth and no scratches can be seen. Be critical. Shine a light directly on to the work. Sometimes a stubborn line or slight blemish will be almost impossible to get rid of with a turning tool. If this is the case, use a fine abrasive on the end of a flexible shaft and gently sand the rotating surface. The final buffing is best carried out on an open-weave buffing wheel.

Glue the insert into the box lid with epoxy resin adhesive. Take care when doing a dry run; if your fit is really spot on, it will be almost impossible to get the insert out again.

When turning is complete, the disc can be prised from the chuck with the blade of a penknife.

A box lid with a cast polyester resin insert about to be fitted. This will give a translucent lid and show off the alternative mother-of-pearl to its best advantage.

Three boxes, one with a translucent mother-of-pearl lid, one with an inlaid disc of alternative ivory and the third with an inserted ring of ivory.

INSERTED RINGS

To make rings from a sheet of alternative material, cut the disc as above. Mount the disc on a glue chuck and turn a ring. Use a parting tool that has been ground down to produce a 1mm thick blade. With this tool it is possible to cut a ring from the side and from the face of the disc to the diameter and thickness required.

Cut a groove accurately in the box lid to match the prepared insert. The effect is enhanced if the wood contrasts strongly with the insert material.

TRANSLUCENT BOX LID

Turn the lid of the box to form a frame, removing the centre wood entirely. Make the mother-of-pearl insert and glue it on the inside of the lid just as you would glaze a picture frame.

INLAID KNOBS

Turning a knob in wood, cutting a recess and inserting a previously turned blank of alternative ivory is a good way to use up scraps left on the glue chuck. Another option is to turn a knob, cut a narrow groove on the face and insert a ring of turned ivory. Care must be taken with both of these designs, to make sure that the recesses are cut to exactly the right size. Use epoxy resin adhesive to glue in any inlays.

> Do not be afraid to try new materials.

— 10 —

ELEVEN EXERCISES

The following exercises are not intended as projects; they have been designed to encourage the reader to set to work with the lathe and have a go. Completing an exercise from start to finish will allow the turner to become familiar with particular techniques and to gain confidence in using miniature tools and equipment. As with all such skills, practice is vital. Mistakes will happen and wood will be flung into the waste bin in frustration but, with perseverance, you should eventually be able to apply the techniques and the skills acquired to your own projects.

The holding methods and techniques described are not necessarily definitive. There are a number of different ways of doing things, and woodturners are usually good at improvising, in order to make maximum use of the equipment they have available and to find solutions to problems. Not everyone will agree with everything here, but these are the methods that work for me.

The exercises use the basic equipment, first to turn spindles between centres and then items on a faceplate, glue chuck, screwchuck and drill chuck. A

Very small bowls turned in laburnum and plum and a bowl and vase made in yew.

combination chuck is introduced and used in both compression and expansion modes. The final exercise is more challenging and uses many of the techniques that have been practised, together with indexing and drilling.

Adopt a flexible approach to your turning but base it on sound and safe techniques.

EXERCISE 1: SPINDLE TURNING BETWEEN CENTRES TO PRODUCE A SCALED-DOWN VICTORIAN TABLE LEG

Aim	To practise spindle turning on a blank held between centres using the skew chisel
Example	A quarter-scale Victorian kitchen-table leg
Equipment	Four-prong drive and a revolving centre
Blank size	Each leg 175 × 18 × 18mm

This spindle-turning exercise practises simple between-centre turning. The leg chosen has a square top, a baluster body, a bead and a shaped foot. Each change of direction is determined with reference to the turning guide. All the turning is carried out with the skew chisel, demonstrating the versatility of this important tool.

1. First produce a turning guide showing the main datum points (*see* the picture above). This is particularly important when producing more than one spindle of the same shape and size – as with table legs.

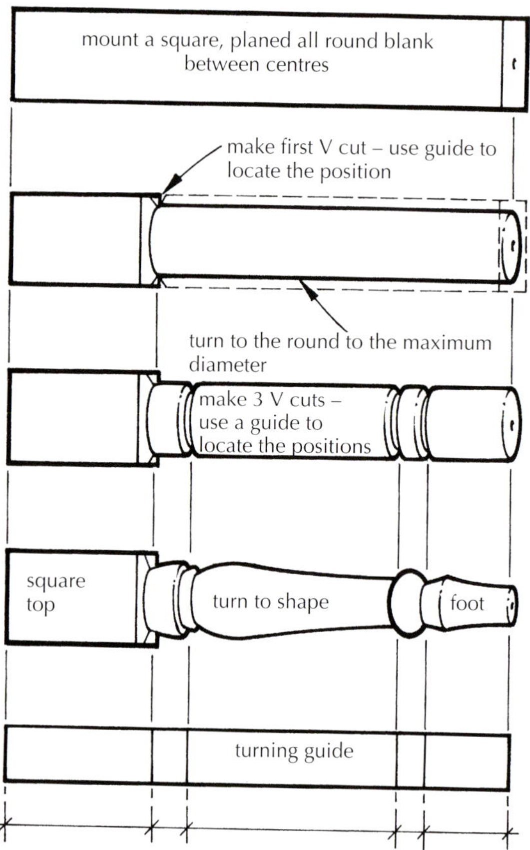

Stages in turning a scaled-down Victorian table leg between centres.

2. Prepare a square-section blank and mark the centres at each end and centre pop.
3. Mount the blank between a four-prong drive and a revolving centre. Apply sufficient pressure with the tailstock to give the blank effective contact with the drive, but avoid excessive pressure, which could result in the wood splitting. For small-diameter work, too much pressure from the tailstock can result in wood whipping in the centre.
4. Set the lathe speed to 2,000rpm and use this speed throughout.
5. Draw in pencil the position of the first V cut, which indicates the start of the round section of the leg below the

Making the first V cut with the long point of the skew. The wood is coloured red for clarity.

Using the turning guide to transfer the markings for the position of the three V cuts.

square shoulder. Using the long point of a 12.5mm oval skew, cut a V and then with the same tool turn the area below the V to the base of the leg to the maximum diameter.

6. Mark the position of, and then cut, the other 3 Vs at the positions shown on the turning guide and turn the leg to shape. Make gentle but positive cuts with the tools and use the forefinger of the left hand under the work to act as a steady. With the lathe stationary, check the spindle diameters using callipers at regular intervals.

Remember: always cut downhill, take your time, and keep the bevel close to the wood.

Practise producing matching spindles at this scale to build confidence, then try reducing the size.

Turning the baluster shape with a 12.5mm oval skew. The left-hand forefinger supports the work.

Producing the bead with an oval skew. The red line shows the top of the bead and will only be removed on the final cut. The cutting is always downhill, with the bevel as close to the wood as possible.

EXERCISE 2: REPETITIVE TURNING BETWEEN CENTRES TO PRODUCE SPINDLES FOR A GALLERY RAIL

Aim	To produce a number of matching spindles
Example	Spindles for a gallery rail
Equipment	A stepped friction drive and a revolving centre
Blank size	Each spindle 70 × 24 × 24mm

Making a gallery rail is a good exercise in repetitive turning. Each blank is held in turn on a stepped friction drive and, when turning is complete, proprietry 6mm dowels are inserted in the holes at either end. This is more satisfactory than turning spigots on the spindles themselves, and it produces a strong rail. The friction drive is a simple and effective way of holding blanks that have been pre-drilled and, if a mistake is made with the tool, the work will stop rotating while the lathe continues to run. This makes the process safer and less alarming when things go wrong. It also means that when the work is finished

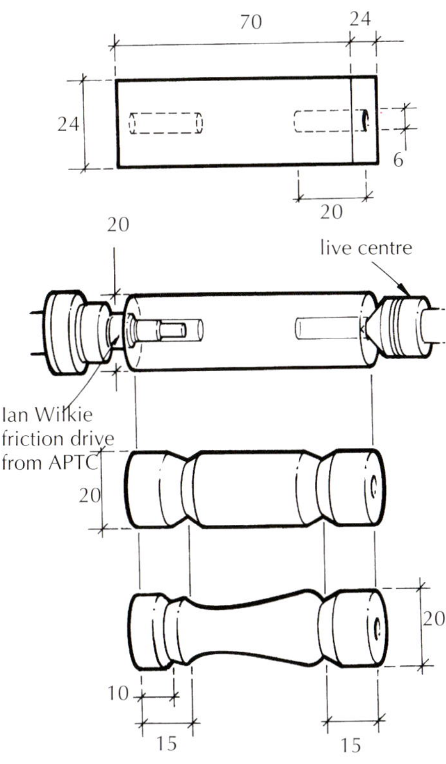

Stages in turning gallery rail spindles.

the hole will be exactly in the centre at both ends.

1. Cut the number of blanks required for the rail and square off the ends accurately; this is very important.
2. Drill a 6mm diameter hole at each end to a depth of 20mm.
3. Mount one blank on the 6mm step of a friction drive fitted in the headstock and bring up a revolving centre to support the other end. Note that a revolving centre must always be used with a friction drive.
4. Turn the blank to a diameter of 20mm with a roughing-out gouge. Mark off 15mm from each end and make two V cuts with the long point of a skew.
5. Form a baluster shape between the two V cuts using a 6mm spindle gouge and always cutting downhill.
6. Mark off 10mm from the headstock end and form the second decorative V cut.
7. Remove the spindle and place the next

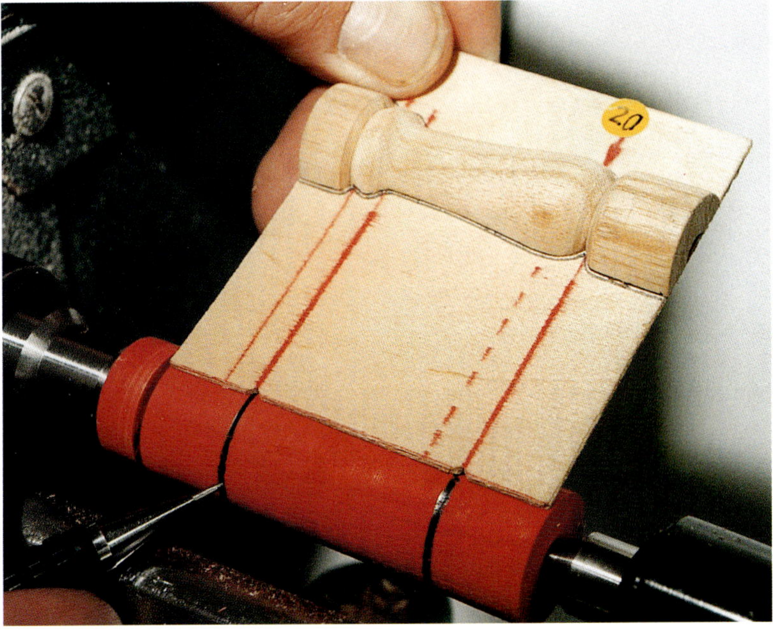

A split-turned spindle turned to act as a guide for the rest of the spindles. The lines are transferred to the blank (painted red). The yellow sticker with '20' written on it refers to the maximum diameter.

A measurement being taken with callipers; the lathe is stationary.

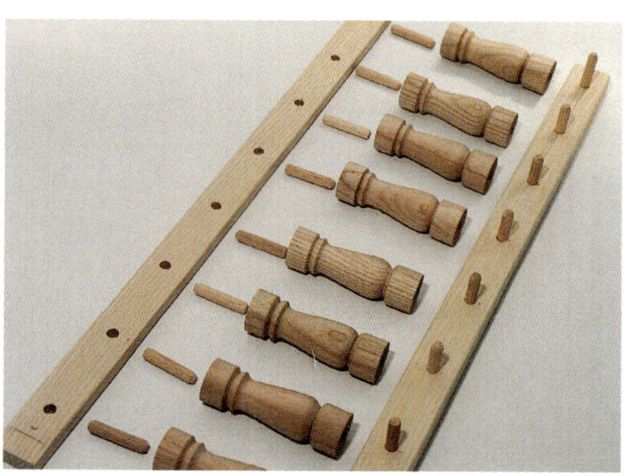

Rails and spindles about to be assembled with proprietary 6mm dowels.

Removing a finished spindle from the stepped friction drive. A matching dowel will be inserted in the hole at each end.

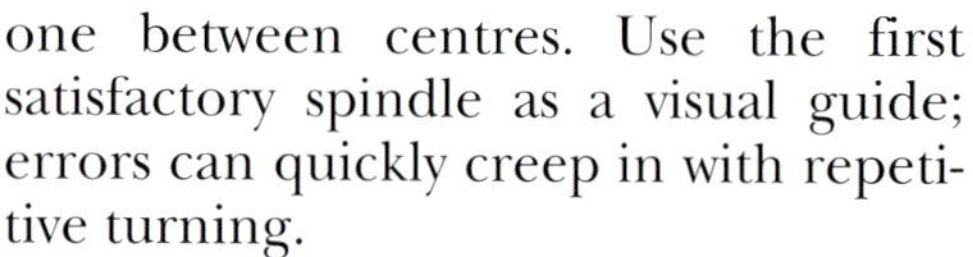

one between centres. Use the first satisfactory spindle as a visual guide; errors can quickly creep in with repetitive turning.

8. When all the spindles have been produced, assemble the rail using proprietary 6mm dowels glued and tapped into the holes at each end.

Finished gallery rail.

EXERCISE 3: PRODUCING A FRAME ON A GLUE CHUCK

Aim	To turn, holding the work on a glue chuck and finishing off on a jam chuck
Example	A small frame to hold a photograph, picture or mirror
Equipment	50mm faceplate and a revolving centre
Blank size	55 × 55 × 50mm

Most lathes come with a faceplate of small diameter and the 50mm size is ideal. Wood can be mounted directly on the faceplate by means of three, four or six countersunk woodscrews. This method is simple, relatively inexpensive and the blank is held very firmly. The disadvantage is that the base of the item turned is left with holes, or, if you choose to part off the wood and make allowance for the ends of the screws, wood is wasted.

One alternative is to use the faceplate as a glue chuck, allowing work to be turned right down to the glue line, with no risk of the turning tool inadvertently coming into contact with the ends of the woodscrews. When working with expensive exotic wood, there is very little wastage. Making a glue chuck is simple and, if it is cleaned off and trued up after use, it can be used again and again. For detailed instructions, *see* Chapter 8.

1. Make a glue chuck for a 50mm faceplate and hot-melt glue the blank to it.
2. Bring up the tailstock fitted with a revolving centre to give support and turn the blank to the round with a roughing-out gouge or a spindle gouge.
3. Withdraw the tailstock and face off the outer surface with a spindle gouge.
4. Cut a recess with a parting tool, or a beading tool, in the front face to a depth that allows for the picture, the glazing and the back piece.
5. Using a very thin parting tool, cut in from the side to a depth of 12mm.
6. Still using the parting tool, cut in from the face, leaving a small rebate until the cut meets the side cut and the frame parts. The back with its rebate is now complete.
7. The outer surface of the frame is smooth but the front face will not have been turned. To hold the frame for the next stage it is necessary to make a jam chuck.
8. Turn a spigot on the remaining wood held on the glue chuck with a diameter to match the internal diameter of the back of the rebate. Turn the spigot with care and check until you have a good snug fit. Push the frame on to the spigot and gently turn the front face to shape.
9. Sand, burnish and polish.
10 The frame can be glazed with a circle cut from a thin sheet of clear acrylic. A back cover may be made from plywood or card.

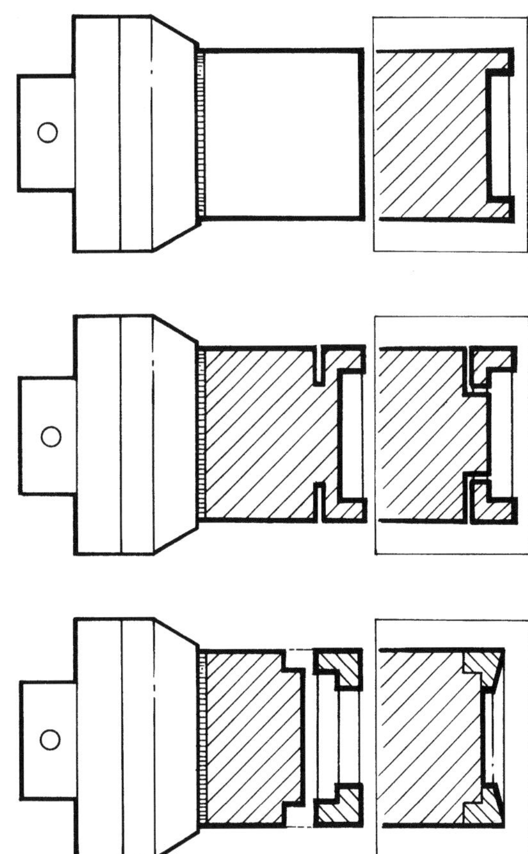

Stages in turning a frame on a glue chuck.

The completed frame removed from the jam chuck.

The finished frame.

EXERCISE 4: TURNING A KNOB ON A DEDICATED SCREWCHUCK

Aim	To turn with the blank mounted on a dedicated screwchuck
Example	A knob
Equipment	A dedicated screwchuck
Blank size	As required; for the pine example shown, 70 × 60 × 60mm

Turned knobs of all shapes and sizes are often required and the turner will want to become proficient at making them. The miniature lathe is excellent for this purpose and the screwchuck is particularly good for turning large and medium-sized knobs; very small knobs are best held by their spigots in a drill chuck or a collet chuck.

The functional design of a knob, which will be frequently handled and pulled, is often overlooked. The top and the waist need to provide a comfortable grip. One suitable shape is the type often found on Victorian chest of drawers (*see* the picture on page 93).

The example was made in pine so that it would stand out well in the picture.

1. Usually, more than one matching knob is required, so it is wise to make a drawing first to determine the correct shape and size. From the drawing, make a turning guide showing the main datum points, and a template for checking the shape of each knob as turning progresses.
2. Prepare a blank slightly larger than the knob required. Mark the centre and centre pop. Some turners like to remove the corners of the blank, particularly when using softwood, to avoid any wood breaking off during the initial turning.
3. Drill a pilot hole to the correct diameter and depth for the screwchuck that is to be used. A plywood spacer placed between the face of the chuck and the blank not only protects the face of the chuck but also reduces the depth of the pilot hole required and this can save wood.
4. Position the toolrest and turn the blank to the round with a roughing-out gouge. Using a spindle gouge, shape the knob from the top to the flange and, with a parting tool, form the spigot. Slightly

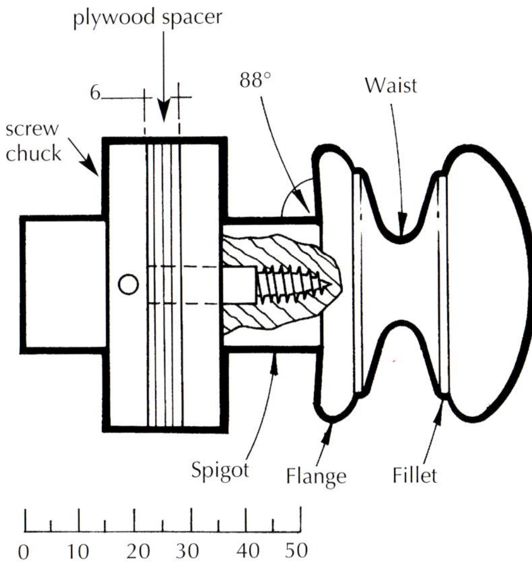

Turning a knob on a dedicated screwchuck.

undercut the underside of the flange so that the knob will fit snugly on to the host item.

5. Stop the lathe from time to time and check the shape with the aid of the template.
6. Sand, burnish and polish the knob as required.

EXERCISE 5: TURNING A CLOCK FINIAL ON A DRILL CHUCK

Aim	Using a drill chuck to hold blanks with a pre-turned spigot
Example	A small clock finial
Equipment	Four-prong drive, revolving centre and a drill chuck
Blank size	To suit the size of finial desired; for this example, 111 × 45 × 45mm

Finials for clocks and other items of furniture can be readily turned on the miniature lathe. If more than one is to be made, a turning guide will ensure that they all look alike. Finials usually have a spigot in the base to fit in a hole in the host item. A drill chuck is an effective way of holding a spigot but tailstock support, by means of a revolving centre, is invariably needed until the very last minute.

1. Cut a blank 10mm larger than the overall length of the finial, to allow for the waste at the tailstock end, and slightly thicker than the maximum diameter required.
2. The first task is to form a spigot that can be held in the drill chuck. Centre pop each end of the blank and mount the wood between centres with a four-prong drive in the headstock and a revolving centre in the tailstock.
3. Turn to the round with a roughing-out gouge and form a spigot with a parting tool 12mm diameter × 15mm long. Slightly undercut the underside of the flange (*see* Exercise 4).
4. Remove the work from the lathe and fit a 13mm capacity drill chuck in the headstock and mount the spigot in the jaws of the drill chuck. Make a small felt pen mark on the underside of the flange and a matching one on the drill chuck. This will aid accurate realignment, should the finial need to be rechucked for any reason. Support the other end of the blank with a revolving centre and then tighten the drill chuck.
5. With a 6mm spindle gouge turn the finial to shape, working from the tailstock end to the headstock leaving 10mm waste wood at the tailstock end. Gently sand and burnish the finial.

Using a turning guide to mark out the datum points on the blank.

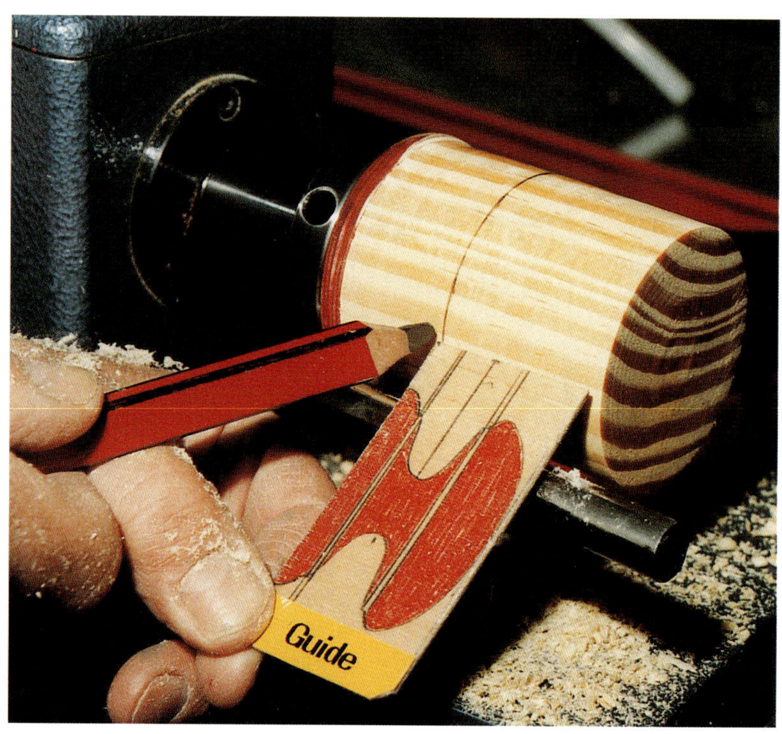

Using a template to check the exact shape of the knob.

Cutting through the remainder of the spigot with a junior hacksaw fitted with a woodcutting blade. It is not good practice to part right through, since the item could fly off. The lathe is stationary during this operation.

The completed pine knob and a selection of other shapes and styles.

Turning a small clock finial using a drill chuck.

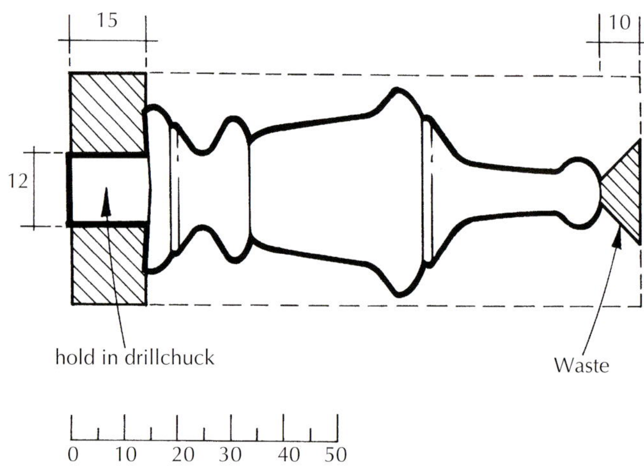

6. With the long point of a skew gently reduce the diameter at the tailstock end of the finial to a minimum of 3mm. Stop the lathe and cut through the remaining wood with a fine saw. Select a slow speed and smooth off the top of the finial with abrasive.
7. Gently sand and burnish the rest of the finial and polish if required.

Completed mahogany clock finial being removed from the drill chuck. The red index mark on the chuck is a shallow hole filled with red paint. Its purpose is to line up with a similar mark put on the knob flange so that the work can be remounted accurately if necessary.

EXERCISE 6: USING THE MICRO CHUCK IN COMPRESSION MODE TO PRODUCE BALL FINIALS

Aim	To turn a small item without tailstock support on a screwchuck insert held in a combination chuck in compression mode
Example	A small ball finial turned in sycamore to top a gatepost for the entrance to an imposing ½in scale dolls' house
Equipment	Micro chuck, MJ35 jaws, SCO4 screwchuck insert
Blank size	25 × 25 × 42mm

The combination of the Micro chuck with the small screw insert held in the jaws. is excellent for turning very small items; the grip is very firm and positive and no tailstock support is necessary. As a result there is complete freedom of movement for the turning tool, with access all round the item being turned.

1. If more than one ball shape is required, prepare a simple template to make sure they are all the same size and shape.
2. Mark the centre at one end of the prepared blank and drill a pilot hole 4mm diameter × 16mm deep. Note that this will be the length of the screw with the sharp point ground off.
3. Fit the micro chuck to the lathe with the MJ35 jaws in position. Mount the screwchuck in the jaws and tighten. Screw on the prepared blank until it is firmly held.
4. Turn the blank to a cylinder 20mm in diameter and face off the end. Using the template, mark lines at 20mm from the end and 10mm.
5. Form the top end of the sphere with a 6mm gouge and a 12.5mm oval skew and then develop the lower end, making sure that the shape is symmetrical. This is where the template comes in; take plenty of time and avoid flats forming.

EXERCISE 7: USING THE MICRO CHUCK IN EXPANSION MODE TO TURN A COASTER

Aim	To prepare a dovetail recess for chuck jaws in expansion mode and to turn a recess for a tile insert
Example	A drinks coaster turned in beech with a 90mm diameter tile insert
Equipment	Micro chuck, MJ35 jaws, SCO4 screwchuck insert, 3mm plywood spacer
Blank size	125mm diameter × 25mm thick

In this exercise the chuck jaws are expanded into a prepared dovetail recess on one face of the blank. It is very important to prepare the recess carefully and accurately to the precise dimensions given by the manufacturer. In the case of the MJ35 jaws, the size of the dovetail recess required is 35mm diameter × 5mm deep. If the dovetail is too large the wood will not be gripped firmly enough and if it is too small it will not be possible to insert the chuck jaws. Making a permanent template for each set of jaws saves a lot of time; keep it with the appropriate set.

After finding the centre of the blank, a 4 x 16mm pilot hole is drilled ready for the SCO4 screwchuck.

Marking the datum lines on the blank using a simple guide. The template shape will be used later to check that each ball turned is completely round.

The completed turning with its square-section base.

Include on the template measurements for the jaws in expansion for a dovetail recess, and in contraction for a dovetail spigot.

1. Drill a centre hole 4mm diameter × 13mm deep in the blank. Place the chuck with the MJ35 jaws in the lathe and secure the SCO4 screwchuck insert (*see* Exercise 6). Cut a 3mm plywood spacer to go between the face of the screwchuck and the blank, to reduce the overall length of the screw, and then mount the blank.
2. With the lathe speed set at 1,500rpm, turn the wood to the round with a 6mm spindle gouge and true off the outer face. With the aid of the template, mark out a 35mm circle and with a parting tool or beading tool, form a recess 5mm deep × 35mm diameter. With the oval skew on its side, form a dovetail, making sure that the inner corners are crisp.
3. Check with the template and then sand and burnish the base and polish if required.
4. Remove the partly turned work from the screwchuck and dismantle the chuck. Reassemble with the MJ35 jaws and the two rings so that the jaws will expand into the prepared dovetail recess when the chuck is tightened.
5. Check that the blank is running true and that it is held securely. If this is not the case, loosen the chuck, rotate the blank by hand and re-tighten; this is often sufficient to correct any inaccuracy.
6. Draw a circle on the blank to match the chosen tile (the smaller tile inserts usually have a diameter of 90mm) and then form the recess to the correct

Checking the turned recess with a template to ensure that it is the correct diameter and depth for the MJ35 jaws.

Mounting the sycamore blank on the MJ35 jaws.

Expanding the jaws by means of the two tommy bars (with red handles).

One completed coaster with a decorative ceramic tile and the second coaster still on the lathe with a turned recess to take a cork tile.

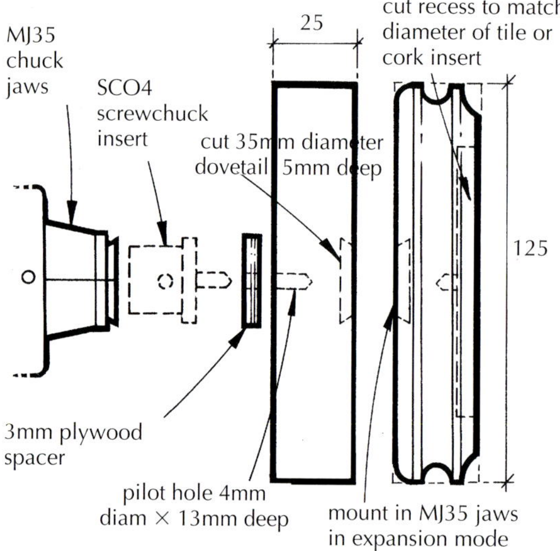

Turning a coaster with the chuck in expansion mode.

diameter and depth with the spindle gouge. Use a spindle gouge to mould the outer edge. Make sure the recess is perfectly flat so that the tile will be level. A 50mm engineer's square is ideal for checking flatness in small recesses. The aim should be to produce a good, but not too tight fit for the tile.

7. Sand, burnish and polish. Do not polish the inside of the recess if the tile is to be glued in permanently otherwise the adhesive will not be effective. Special silicon-based adhesives that remain flexible are available to glue tiles and mirrors in position; they allow the wood to expand and contract without cracking the tile.

EXERCISE 8: TURNING A SMALL BOWL WITH THE CHUCK JAWS IN COMPRESSION MODE

Aim	To prepare a dovetail spigot and turn an item held by the spigot in compression mode and to use jam chucking to remove the spigot
Example	A small bowl turned in elm
Equipment	Micro chuck, MJ35 jaws in compression mode, SCO4 screwchuck insert
Blank size	100mm diameter × 40mm thick

Small bowls and platters can be turned up to the maximum size that the lathe can handle. In this example, 170mm was the largest diameter possible on the Selbix Mini lathe. The bowl is turned in two stages. During the first stage, the blank is held on the screwchuck so that a dovetail spigot can be formed and the outside of the bowl completed. During the second stage, the partly turned bowl is held by its spigot in the chuck jaws and the inside is turned.

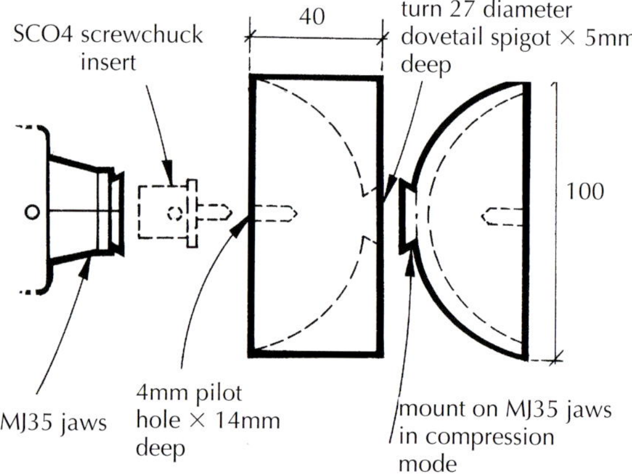

Turning a small bowl with the chuck jaws in compression mode.

1. Drill a central pilot hole in the blank 4mm diameter × 14mm deep and mount the blank on the screwchuck (*see* Exercise 6). Do not use a plywood spacer, because the area where the hole is drilled will be completely removed in the second stage of turning. Check that the blank is held firmly and that it rotates without obstruction.
2. Set the lathe speed to 1,500rpm and true off the outer face using a 6mm spindle gouge. Form a parallel spigot with a parting tool 27mm diameter × 5mm long.
3. Use the template produced for Exercise 7 to check that the measurements are correct. Undercut the spigot to form a dovetail using a 12mm skew on its side. If this technique is to be used often, grind a spare miniature scraper just for forming dovetails.
4. Form the outer shape of the bowl with a 6mm spindle gouge, taking gentle cuts and flowing right through the curve until the desired shape has been achieved.
5. Sand and burnish. Complete the polishing of the outside surface of the bowl before removing it from the screwchuck. When the partly turned bowl is remounted on the dovetail spigot, and the inside has been hollowed out, the outside surface may not remain completely round. As a result, trying to apply friction polish later to the outside will probably result in an uneven finish.
6. Unscrew the partly turned bowl and remove the screwchuck. Reverse the blank, compress the chuck jaws on to the dovetail spigot and lock firmly. Use the chuck in compression mode whenever possible – it is unnecessary to remove the chuck from the lathe and no alteration to its configuration is needed.
7. Chamfer the outer edge with a 6mm gouge first, to form the lip of the bowl. If the chamfering is left until the bowl has been hollowed out, there is always a chance that the gouge might catch the rim and ruin all the hard work.
8. Begin hollowing out at the centre, still using the same gouge, in even sweeps, with the bevel close to the wood. Continue in this way until the final shape has been achieved. The gouge must be kept sharp and this will involve stopping the work to hone the tool from time to time. Beginners tend to produce clumsy bowls with interrupted curves, usually because of a reluctance to turn a really thin wall. These small bowls, however, need to be quite delicate, so be brave! One of the advantages of turning in miniature is that a broken bowl is not too much of a disaster. The rotating edge of a bowl can be quite sharp, so stop the lathe before touching the work to see how thin the wall is.
9. Sand, burnish and polish the inside and rim of the bowl to match the outside.
10. Remove the bowl from the chuck jaws. Now, either leave the spigot on the base of the bowl, to give the bowl a slightly oriental look, or turn the foot off.
11. To turn the foot off, make a jam chuck from a piece of scrap wood mounted on the screwchuck. Measure the rim of the bowl, add an extra 20mm and turn the jam chuck to this total diameter. Turn a recess 5mm deep with a diameter to match the rim of the bowl. Gently press the bowl into the recess and bring up the tailstock fitted with a revolving centre to hold it in position. Using the gouge, gently turn off the foot until there is just enough wood left around the revolving centre. Remove the bowl from the jam chuck and pare off

Using the template to check the diameter of the turned dovetail spigot on the partly turned bowl.

The spigot held in the MJ35 jaws in compression. The inside of the bowl has been hollowed out and is ready for sanding.

The finished bowl with its dovetail-shaped foot left on.

A jam chuck made from MDF with a turned groove to support the rim of the bowl.

The bowl held in the groove of the jam chuck by means of tailstock pressure from a revolving centre so that the foot can be turned off with a 6mm spindle gouge.

any remaining wood with a small chisel. Sand and polish the base.

EXERCISE 9: TURNING A BOX USING A CHUCK

Aim	To prepare a blank from branchwood and to turn a box with the smaller chuck jaws in compression and then jam chuck to finish
Example	A small pillbox turned in yew
Equipment	Micro chuck, quick-release carrier, ring centre, MJ25 jaws in compression mode
Blank size	To suit the capacity of the lathe and the timber available; for the example shown, yew branchwood 80mm long × 45mm diameter

Learning to turn a box is a good discipline and there are many ways to do it. This method ensures that, when the lid is on the box, the grain matches up. A good box should stay together if it is lifted by the lid. The outside of the box can be shaped, carved or decorated with inlays – the possibilities are endless. Turning boxes is well within the scope of the miniature lathe and many woodturners specialize in this aspect of the craft.

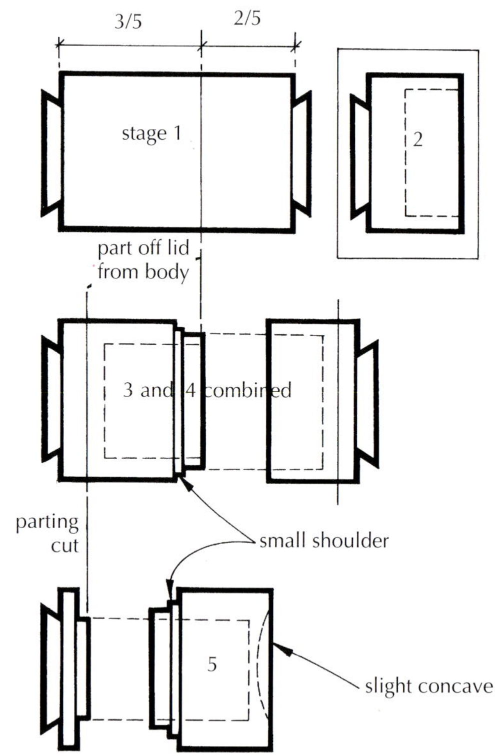

Turning box using a chuck.

1. First, the branchwood, or the blank needs to be turned to the round between centres. Here the ring centre is held by its MT shank in the quick-release carrier, which in turn is held in the chuck. A revolving centre is positioned in the tailstock. The lathe speed is set at 2,500 rpm. Spigots are turned at either end of the cylinder. The MJ25 jaws selected for this project compress on to a 21mm × 5mm long dovetail spigot and this makes them ideal for holding a small blank to turn a pillbox of 35mm diameter; use larger jaws for larger boxes. Part the lid from the body.
2. Mount the lid in the chuck jaws by means of the spigot. Hollow out the inside and then remove the lid from the chuck.
3. Hold the body in the chuck by its dovetail spigot and cut a further spigot at the other end to form a jam chuck to hold the lid. Reverse the lid on to the jam chuck, turn off the dovetail and sand and polish the top. The lid is now complete and may be removed from the jam chuck.
4. Hollow out the body of the box and cut a second very small shoulder on the outer edge. When the lid is in position on the completed box, this secondary

Checking the dovetail spigots with Vernier callipers with the lathe stationary.

Reversing the lid and pushing it on to the jam chuck turned at the end of the body.

recess disguises the fact that the grain does not match up precisely because some of the wood has been removed during parting off.

5. Sand and polish the inside before parting off, leaving some waste wood in the chuck jaws.
6. Turn a spigot on the remaining wood, to form a jam chuck for the body. Push the body on and true up the base before turning the base slightly concave so that it sits firmly on its outside rim.
7. Sand and polish the outside and the base. The grain on the lid should match up with the grain on the base.

Hollowing out the body with the beading tool. The turned secondary shoulder is clearly visible. The jaws grip the dovetail spigot in compression very firmly.

Checking the depth of the box with a dedicated depth gauge. Stop the lathe when checking to avoid damaging the rim of the box.

Parting off the body. The parting tool has a ground end, to reduce its thickness, so that it can be used to form a slightly concave bottom surface.

EXERCISE 10: TURNING A HOLLOW FORM BOTTLE

Aim	To turn a hollow form in two parts with the body held in chuck jaws in compression and using miniature hook tools for hollowing out
Example	Hollow form bottle
Equipment	Craft Supplies Minigrip 1000 chuck with the standard jaws in compression
Blank size	Body: 60 × 60 × 100mm Neck: 40mm diameter × 45mm thick

This little hollowed-out bottle is made in two parts; in the example the body is turned in cherry and the neck in rosewood, but any two contrasting woods will be effective. The finished bottle is 90mm high and the maximum diameter is 60mm.

1. Mount the body blank on a screw chuck and give tailstock support. Turn a cylinder and produce a dovetail spigot at one end to suit the chuck jaws you are going to use. In the example shown the Craft Supplies Minigrip chuck was used and the dovetail required measured 37.5 × 5mm.
2. Mount the blank on the chuck and face off. Insert a drillchuck in the tailstock and drill a hole 60mm deep, using a 25mm saw-tooth Forstner bit.
3. Support the blank with a revolving centre fitted with a large point. If you do not have an interchangeable revolving centre, turn up a plug to fill the hole temporarily.
4. Turn the outside of the bottle to shape, leaving a 4mm flat at the edge of the hole.
5. After sanding remove the tailstock completely to give plenty of room to manoeuvre for hollowing out the inside. Use a hook tool and stop frequently to clear out the shavings and to check the wall thickness. Leave a 2mm long, parallel-sided 25mm diameter entry hole to take the neck spigot.
6. Remove the chuck from the lathe but leave the partly-turned bottle in the jaws.

Using a chuck template to mark off the size of the spigot required.

Checking the depth of the hole with a depth gauge.

Hollowing out the bottle with a Henry Taylor miniature hook tool.

7. Mount a blank for the neck on a screw chuck and turn the wood to a diameter of 35mm. Drill a 6mm diameter hole to a depth of 25mm with a drill mounted in the tailstock.
8. Turn a 25mm diameter × 2mm long spigot on the outboard end of the blank to fit snugly into the previously turned body and check for a good fit. Turn the waist with a spindle gouge, taking care to cut downhill and to avoid the wings catching the sides. Bring the body up to the turning from time to time to see that the curve at the top of the bottle flows into the curve of the top. Gently form the inner curve.
9. When you are satisfied, sand and burnish the work and use a thin parting tool to part off the neck at an angle to form a recess in the top, sloping towards the centre hole.
10. Put the chuck holding the partly turned body back on the lathe and glue on the neck, bringing up the tailstock and a revolving centre to act as a cramp. Wipe away any excess glue immediately before it can stain the wood. Using a small spindle gouge, gently finish off the top surface of the neck.
11. Apply cellulose sanding sealer followed by friction polish and finally a coat of wax.
12. Part off with a thin parting tool, slightly undercutting so that the bottle will stand on its outer rim.

Parting off the finished bottle.

EXERCISE 11: SUGAR OR SPICE SIFTER

Aim	To practise dovetail, jam and glue chucking, hollowing out, indexing and drilling
Example	A sugar or spice sifter in the style of around 1750
Equipment	Friction drive, revolving centre with cone accessory. Micro chuck, MJ 45 jaws, MJ 35 jaws. Flexible drive and 2 and 2.5mm twist drills
Blank size	Body blank 100 × 65 × 65mm; foot blank 65mm diameter × 25mm thick; top blank 70 × 40 × 40mm; alternative ivory rod 40mm diameter × 40mm long

Sifters for sugar and spice, sometimes described as 'muffineers', were often made in fruitwood, *lignum vitae* and silver in the eighteenth and nineteenth century. Even though it is unlikely to be used, this item of treen is interesting and challenging to turn, and brings together a number of the techniques practised in the previous exercises. Various parts go together to make this item (*see* the picture on page 113); this example was made from walnut, boxwood and alternative ivory. The finished sifter is 150mm high but it can be scaled down without too much trouble (*see* the picture on page 117). It is even possible to make a minute one for the dolls' house, but beware – it can easily disappear in the shavings!

BODY

1. Turn a dovetail spigot on the body blank to suit the chuck jaws being used. Mount the body blank on the chuck and, with tailstock support, turn

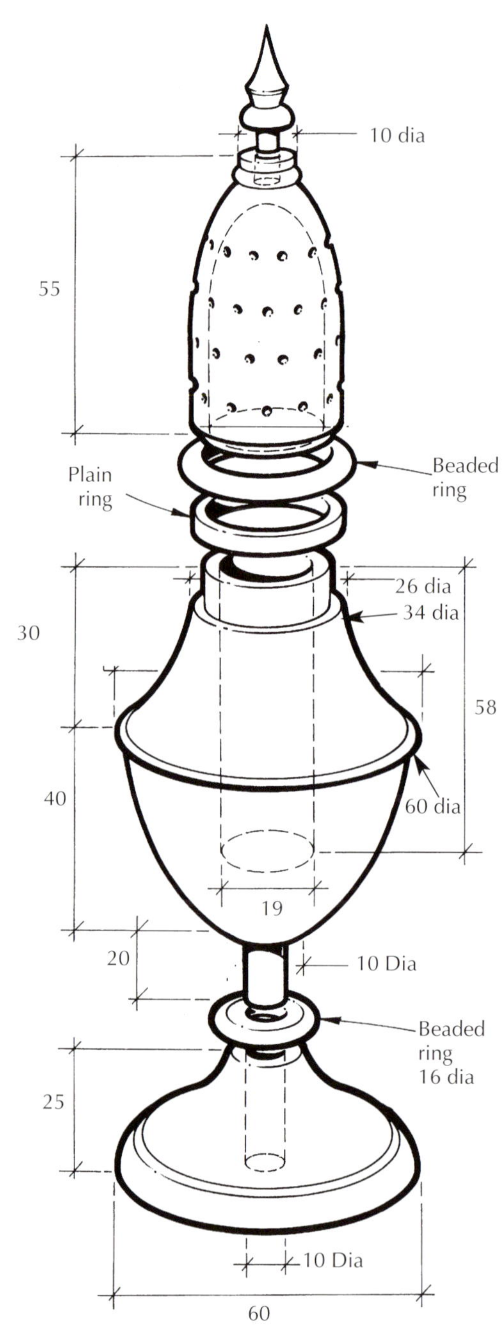

Dimensions for a sugar or spice sifter, also showing the parts for a sifter.

Checking the diameters of the body with the plan. A multi-head revolving centre has been fitted with a large-diameter cone to support the rim of the top of the body. If a multi-head is not being used, turn a wooden plug to act in the same way as the cone.

Burnishing the walnut foot with Hermes Webrax non-woven web abrasive.

Checking that the body fits the top.

Drilling the marked indexed holes with a fine drill held in the chuck of a flexible drive. The top is supported by a cone accessory fitted in the multi-head revolving centre.

to produce a cylinder of 60mm diameter.
2. Move back the tailstock, reposition the toolrest and begin to hollow out, aiming to leave sufficient wood at the base and sides so that the body has weight. Shape from the tailstock end, gradually working towards the headstock.
3. Form the shoulder, making sure it is absolutely parallel.
4. Finally turn a spigot 10mm diameter × 20mm at the base and part off.

FOOT

1. Drill the centre of the foot blank right through with a 9.9mm drill bit.
2. Mount the blank on a stepped friction drive; the 9.9mm hole will ensure a good tight fit on the 10mm step. Bring up a revolving centre fitted with a cone end, which will ensure that the wood is not marked.
3. Turn the foot to shape.

TOP

1. Prepare a dovetail spigot at one end of the blank and centre pop the other end.
2. Mount the spigot in the MJ35mm chuck jaws and turn the blank to a diameter of 34mm, giving tailstock support.
3. Remove the tailstock and begin to hollow out with a beading tool and a small round-nosed scraper and then shape the outer form with a 6mm spindle gouge.
4. Turn the shoulder accurately. This will later take the beaded ring of alternative ivory. The inside of the top is designed to fit snugly over the body, so check regularly for a good fit.
5. Make a jam chuck from a scrap of wood held on a faceplate, or in the chuck jaws, and push on the top of the sifter.
6. Fit a drill in the tailstock and drill a central 2.5 × 6mm deep hole to take the finial.
7. Mark four concentric circles approximately 10mm apart on the wood using a soft pencil. Isolate the lathe and use the indexing system of the lathe or chuck to mark twelve positions on the first and third pencilled circles – in other words, every other hole. Offset the second and fourth rings and again mark twelve positions.
8. Fit a 2mm drill into a chuck on a flexible drive and carefully drill the forty-eight holes free hand at the marked positions.
9. Remove any pencil marks with an eraser and gently sand.

RINGS AND FINIAL

1. Turn one flat ring and two beaded rings from one rod of alternative ivory held on a glue chuck. Use a beading tool to turn and a modified thin parting tool to part off.
2. One flat ring sits on the shoulders of the body, one beaded ring sits on the shoulders of the top and the smallest beaded ring fits on the spigot between the body and the foot.
3. Great care needs to be taken to make sure each ring is the correct size. The two rings on the shoulders act as washers and stop the wood moving. The one on the top is formed as a bead so that it can be gripped and the sprinkler top can be removed for refilling.
4. Turn a small finial with a 2.5mm spigot from the remainder of the rod.

FINISH AND ASSEMBLY

1. Polish the various parts. In this example, only the walnut foot was sealed, with cellulose sanding sealer,

while it was still on the lathe. Before assembly, both the walnut foot and the boxwood top and body were buffed and polished on an open-weave calico wheel using carnauba wax to produce a deep lustre.

2. Glue the beaded ring to the shoulders of the sprinkler top and glue the finial in position.
3. Glue the flat ring to the shoulders of the body. Place the small beaded ring over the spigot on the body and then glue the foot in position.

The three rings and finial turned from artificial ivory rod.

Three sifters, in different scales, turned in boxwood, walnut and artificial ivory.

— 11 —

TURNING JEWELLERY

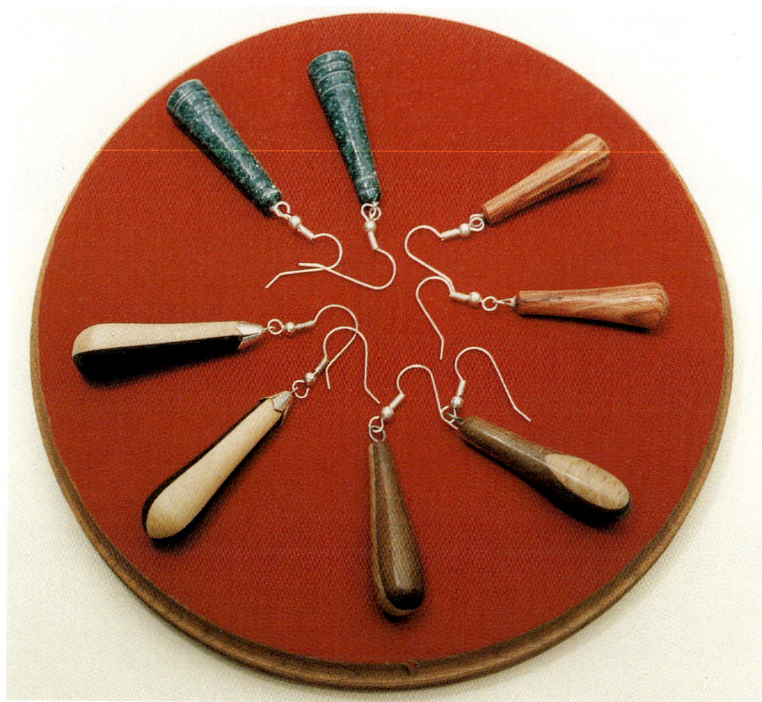

Earrings turned in wood and Corian. If two woods in contrasting colours are laminated together to form a blank, attractive effects are produced when the blank is turned.

Making wooden jewellery offers the woodturner the chance to use small pieces of unusual and exotic wood and may well be of particular interest to women. Only too often the impression is given that woodturning is just a hobby for men, lady turners being very much in the minority at the moment although happily the numbers are increasing. Miniature lathes do not intimidate and are much quieter and more friendly to use.

MATERIALS AND FITTINGS

Many interesting woods, both home-grown and exotic, can be used to good effect in jewellery pieces, either as they are, laminated for interesting pattern and contrast, coloured with stains or paints, or carved and engraved. Some specialist companies sell packs of selected, prepared wood from all over the world, usually described as pen or lace bobbin blanks and measuring 150mm long × 13mm square. One blank could be used for turning a pair of earrings, for example.

Sometimes, mixed bags of exotic wood offcuts are also offered; with luck they might include such varieties as tulipwood, kingwood, ebony and *Piquia amerillo.* Artificial materials such as Corian, cast polyester resin and crushed velvet can all be used in jewellery making with great success.

Jewellery fittings, such as wires for earrings, attachments for pendants, chains, hair clips and brooch pins, are widely available from craft suppliers.

DROP EARRINGS

These earrings fitted with 0.5mm diameter hooked silver wires that can be found at most craft suppliers are designed for pierced ears. If the plan is to turn a large number of identical-sized earrings, it is well worth making a simple turning guide before starting the project.

1. Mount a 75 × 10 × 10mm blank in a set of MJ20 jaws for the Micro chuck with 50mm of wood extending beyond the jaws. Bring up the tailstock fitted with a small revolving centre to give support to the blank.
2. Set the lathe speed to 2,500rpm and turn the blank to the round with a 12.5mm miniature oval skew chisel.

Turned drop earrings.

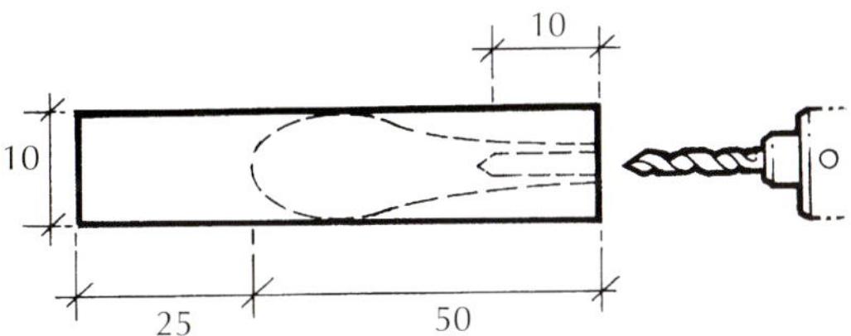

Turning a drop earring.

3. Begin to shape the earring with the narrow end towards the tailstock. Partially turn the bottom of the earring, at the headstock end, leaving sufficient waste wood to reduce the risk of chatter or vibration when sanding. Use callipers regularly to check the diameter and length according to the turning guide, if there is one.
4. Sand and burnish the work.
5. Replace the revolving centre with a 6mm drill chuck held in the tailstock and insert a 1mm twist drill. Start the lathe with a reduced speed of 1,500 rpm and drill a hole to a depth of 10mm in the end of the earring to take the hanging wire.
6. Advance the tailstock by hand, withdrawing the drill from time to

Drilling a fine hole in the end of a drop earring for the wire fitting.

time to clear the shavings. Because the flutes are so small in fine drills they can become clogged very quickly, causing them to break.

7. Remove the drill chuck and move the tailstock back out of the way.
8. Complete the shaping of the bottom end of the earring with the skew until it is parted off. Using 400-grit paper, gently hand sand off any unevenness left on the parting-off area.
9. Produce a matching earring in exactly the same way.
10. Place a drill chuck with a 1MT shank in the headstock spindle, together with a draw-bar. Fit a polishing mop with a 6mm shank pigtail into the drill chuck and screw on a stitched mop. Apply some wax polish to the wood and, with the lathe speed set at 2,000 rpm, polish the bottom end of the earring until it is smooth and shiny.
11. Replace the stitched mop with a loose-leaf mop and polish the whole item; keep the wood moving and rotating all the time.
12. Wire up the earring by passing a length of 0.5mm silvered wire through the hole in the bottom of a hanging earring wire. Twist the ends together and insert them into the drilled hole, securing with superglue or epoxy resin.

PENDANT

This attractive and unusual pendant, designed to hang on a neck chain, consists of two separate turned thin discs each with a convex outer surface and a concave inner surface. There is a small flat edge at the outer circumference for glueing the two discs together (*see* the picture above). The hollowing out reduces the overall weight of the item. Use an attractive figured wood such as olive, laburnum or yew and allow the design to show off the material to its best advantage.

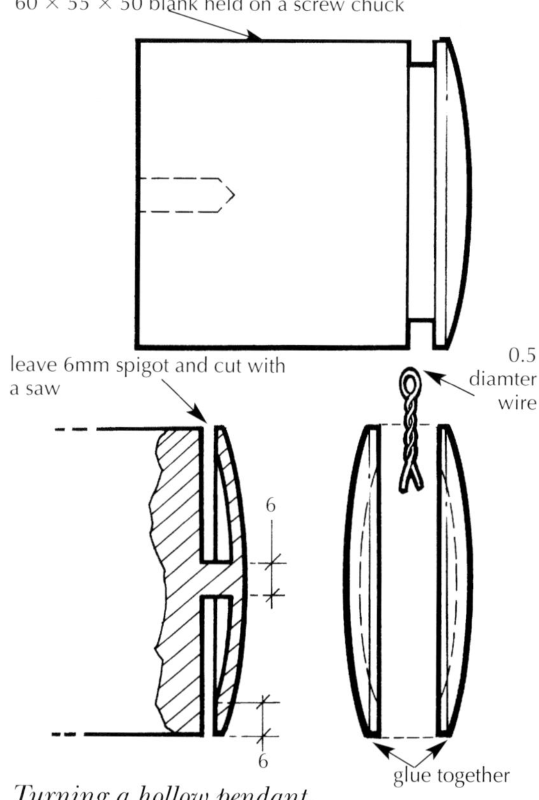

Turning a hollow pendant.

Matching earrings can be made in exactly the same way, reducing the diameter a little. The thinness of the disc very much depends on the skill of the turner but the job will require a really thin parting tool.

1. Prepare a blank 60mm long × 50 × 50mm and mount it on a screwchuck. A blank this size should provide enough wood for four discs, or two pendants. To reduce the depth of the pilot hole, and save wood, use a 6mm plywood disc between the blank and the face of the screwchuck.
2. Set the lathe to 2,000rpm and turn the blank to the round with a roughing-out gouge. Use callipers to check that the diameter is 48mm and that the blank is

parallel. Reset the toolrest and use a sharp 6mm diameter spindle gouge to turn the convex outer form to a dome shape.

3. Sand and burnish the wood and apply polish as desired.
4. Cut a groove 6mm deep, 3mm in from the edge with a parting tool. Widen this groove towards the headstock to give room for manoeuvre. Now, using a thin parting tool, begin a series of cuts to form a matching concave inside face. Continue until the central spigot is reduced to a diameter of about 6mm. The 6mm flat area around the circumference should not be removed.
5. The finish of the underside of the disc should be carefully done but, as the two discs will be glued together, this surface will not be seen. If the spigot is reduced until it parts off too close to the inner surface of the disc, there is a chance that the wood will tear out, leaving a hole in the centre. To be absolutely sure that this does not happen, stop the lathe, cut through the remaining wood with a junior hacksaw and pare off the stub that is left on the back of the disc with a small carving gouge.
6. Using the wood remaining on the screwchuck, produce a second disc in the same way.
7. Buff both discs on a loose-leaf polishing mop with wax polish, keeping the wood moving.
8. Fashion a simple hanging loop from 0.5mm diameter silver jewellery wire. Use a pair of small round-nosed pliers, or the shank of a 3mm twist drill as a former.
9. Look carefully at the discs and decide which way the pendant is to hang. Cut small grooves in the inside rim of both discs to take the twisted wire loop and then glue the parts together with epoxy resin, with the wire loop firmly held inside. Finally, thread a thin silver chain through the loop.

Using a thin Crown parting tool to undercut the concave inner surface. There is enough of the attractive olivewood to make two pendants or one pair of earrings.

TURNING RINGS

Woods with attractive grain, laminated woods and cast polyester resin can all be

Gluing the two halves of an olivewood pendant together with the twisted wire hook inside.

used for making rings. The possibilities for decoration are unlimited, with facets and grooves drilled to take fine dowels of contrasting woods or silver or copper wire. Before turning a ring, measure the finger on which it is to be worn. If a number of rings are to be made, for sale at a craft fair, for example, a ring gauge is inexpensive and useful.

1. Make up a glue chuck mounted on a small faceplate or screwchuck and taper the outer end down to 30mm diameter. Face off, so that the surface is absolutely flat.
2. Hot-melt glue a 40 × 30 × 30mm blank to the glue chuck and then turn it to the round.
3. With a 4mm beading tool, hollow out the blank to a depth just deeper than the width of the ring and to the internal diameter required. Round off the outer edges, sand and then part off using a thin parting tool.
4. Make a jam chuck from the wood remaining on the glue chuck and taper the spigot slightly from front to back. Do not make the spigot too long, as this might hinder access to the inner edge of the ring. Reverse the partly turned ring and push it on to the jam chuck so that the other edges can be rounded off and sanded.
5. Remove the ring and polish it on a loose-leaf buffing wheel.

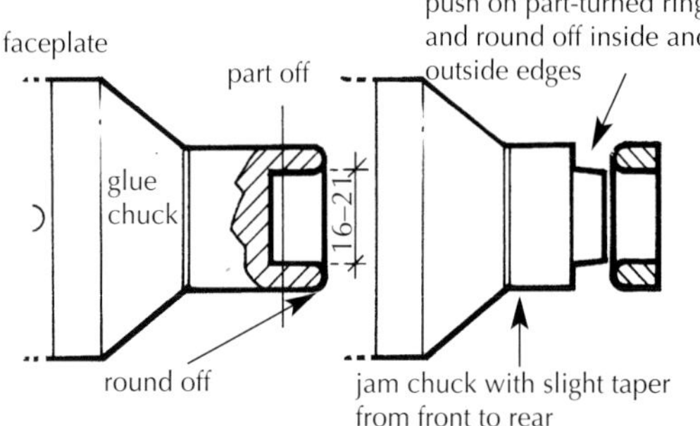

Making rings.

TURNING BEADS

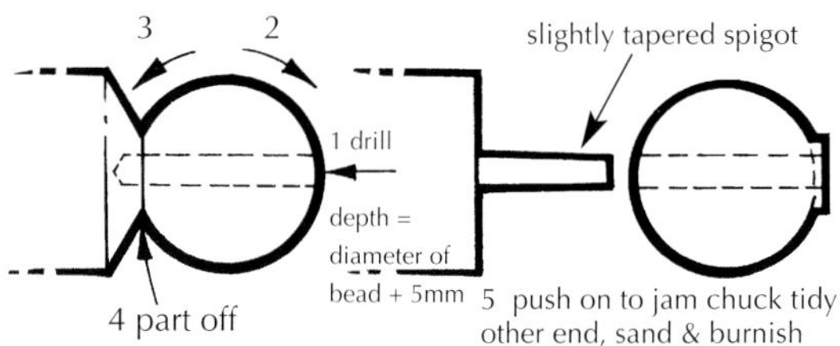

Turning beads.

Attractive and highly decorated wooden, glass and plastic beads are easily available and inexpensive to buy, but the effort of turning them is worth considering. The technique is interesting and beads have uses other than jewellery; *see* the picture on page 123, of a little doll's swing made to hang in my granddaughter's bedroom.

Some turners choose to turn the beads between centres, along a cylinder, like a row of sausages and then drill the individual beads when they have been parted off. The alternative is to make the beads individually and drill them in the lathe; although this method may be slower, it ensures that the hole is always dead centre.

For a large number of identical beads, make a little gauge so that they all end up the same size.

1. Start by preparing lengths of round stock. Hold a blank on a screwchuck, a glue chuck or in the jaws of a micro chuck. Fit a drill chuck in the tailstock and drill a central hole in the pre-turned blank to a depth equal to the diameter of the bead required, plus 5mm.
2. Shape the outer part of the bead with a skew chisel or a small gouge.
3. Begin to shape the inner end of the bead, making sure that the actual shape is symmetrical.

This little novelty swing for a tiny doll involved turning a number of beads.

4. Part off. Repeat the entire process as required.
5. Make a jam chuck out of hardwood (a scrap of boxwood is ideal), with the spigot slightly tapered from the front end to the back and 5mm less than the diameter of the bead. Push a bead on to the spigot so that the parted-off end can be tidied up and sanded.

— 12 —

PEN MAKING

Turning pen barrels and assembling pens is a popular hobby with many woodturners and the choice of colourful and interesting blanks, together with kits of parts to make twist pens, pencils, rollerballs and fountain pens, has expanded to meet increasing interest. A pen can be produced relatively quickly and makes an attractive and personal gift.

The miniature lathe is ideal for pen making and range of equipment needed is quite modest. The author's 12.5mm oval skew from Craft Supplies is all you need to turn simple pens.

A *pen mandrel* is designed to give support to the brass-tubed blanks during turning and the bushes give a guide to the final diameter needed. The 1MT shank is held in the headstock and the blank is supported at the tailstock end with a revolving centre. There are a number of different designs but one of the best

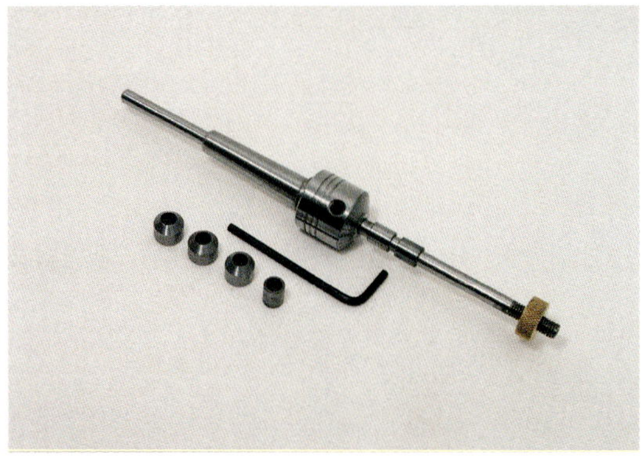

The Planet expanding pen mandrel allows two barrels to be turned at a time. A selection of guide bushes are shown to match two sizes of pen diameter.

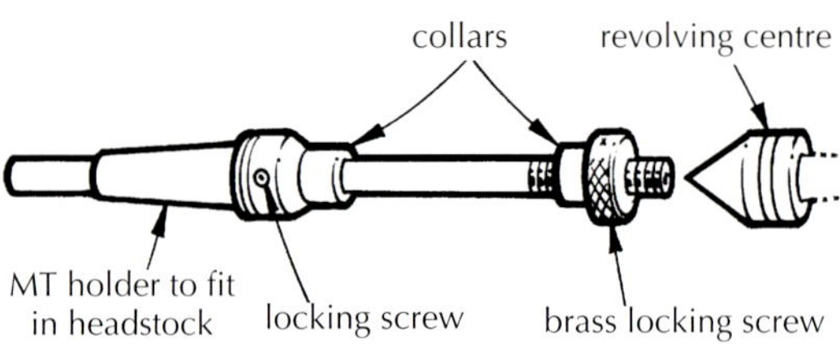

Pen mandrel.

consists of a 1MT carrier, which holds a central 6.2mm rod that can be lengthened or extended as required, to turn one or two blanks at a time. The end of the rod does not have a screw-locking device; instead, it has a conical slide-on end, which secures the blanks by means of pressure from the tailstock revolving centre. This is a quicker device to use than one relying on a locking screw and is ideal for the rapid production of a number of pens.

Pen blanks are available in a wide choice of exotic woods with interesting grain patterns and offer a good opportunity to try out some really beautiful woods in an inexpensive way. The popular Dymondwood blanks come in many exciting colours. Made from natural 1.5mm maple or beech hardwood veneers, they are impregnated with resin and permanently coloured with dyes. The veneers are then bonded at high temperatures and under pressure to form a multi-layered wood product that can be turned, machined and polished.

It is also possible to cut blanks rather than buying them ready-made; the sample pen on page 129 was made from a blank cut from burr elm.

Blanks of elm burr prepared ready to be cut in half. The white correcting fluid is excellent for marking the blanks so that the grain can be matched up again.

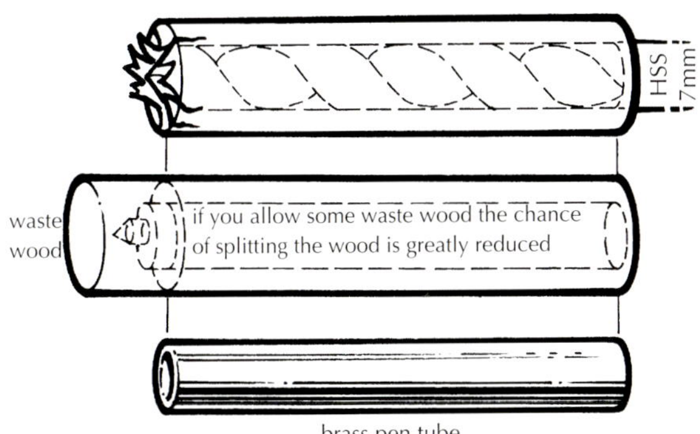

Drilling pen blanks.

TURNING A 7MM TWIST PEN

This type and size of pen is a good starting point in pen making. Basically, the 7mm twist pen is a brass tube glued into a wooden or synthetic blank, which is then turned on a mandrel to the desired diameter. The '7mm' refers to the diameter of the hole that needs to be drilled in the blank to take the brass tube. Buy a pen kit containing all the mechanical parts – there are plenty of kits to choose from, varying in quality and price. Each brand of pen insert is slightly different and it is essential to check the diameter and length of the brass tube before cutting and drilling the blank.

1. Cut an accurate blank 127 × 14 × 14mm or buy a pen blank, which may well be up to 19mm square.
2. Draw a line at the half-way point along the blank at 63.5mm and mark each side of the line in some way so that the grain can be matched up again. Cut the blank in half and mark the centrepoint on the cut face; gently centre pop.
3. Drill a 7mm diameter hole to a depth equalling the length of the brass tube insert in the pen kit, plus 5mm. To drill the hole, hold the blank vertically in a machine vice bolted on to the drillstand table. Many small bench drills have a limited stroke length, which makes drilling a deep hole a problem but an electric drill held in a drillstand usually gives sufficient stroke length. Do not go right through the end of the blank because there is a risk that the wood

will split as the drill breaks through; an HSS bullet twist bit produces a good clean hole.

4. Cut off the waste wood to give a blank length equal to the length of the brass tube insert, plus 2mm. You should now have two blanks, each with a hole right through.
5. Clean the outer surfaces of the brass tubes with fine abrasive and then glue the tubes into the blanks making sure that the adhesive is applied evenly in the hole to give a firm hold. An epoxy two-part adhesive is gap-filling, odourless and reasonably economical; some pen makers prefer thick superglue and an activator. Apply the glue to the inside surface of the hole with a thin bamboo skewer, taking care not to get glue into the tube itself. A short length of 6mm dowel temporarily pushed into the tube before glue is applied keeps the inside clean. Another option is to push the end of the tube into a raw potato or apple and pull it out again! This leaves a plug inside the tube, which stops the adhesive entering.
6. When the adhesive has set, square off the ends of the blanks using a small disc sander or a home-made sander, or a special pen mill. Remove any glue that has entered the inside of the tubes with a 6mm fine rasp or the pen mill, which is designed for this task.
7. Transfer the markings from the sides of the blanks to the end faces, down to the tube, to assist matching up the grain later.
8. Take a pen mandrel and three bushes that match the diameter of the centre ring in the pen kit. Place the mandrel in the headstock MT. Slide on the first bush followed by one blank, the second bush and then the second blank. Finally, slide on the third bush and screw on the locking nut. Bring up the tailstock fitted with a revolving centre to support the outboard end of the mandrel.
9. Set the lathe speed to 2,000rpm, position the toolrest and begin to turn the two blanks to the round with a 12.5mm oval skew.
10. Do not hurry the turning; continually check with a micrometer or Vernier callipers to achieve accuracy and use a straight edge to see that both blanks are truly parallel. The oval skew is the only tool needed throughout the turning; keep it sharp with regular

Waste wood being cut from the pen blanks. The two brass tubes are about to be glued in the blanks with Araldite or superglue. Clean the outside of the tubes first with abrasive. Note that the white marks put on to aid matching the grain are now cut in half.

A home-made sanding disc and table is ideal for truing up the ends of the blanks before turning.

A 12.5mm oval skew, designed by the author and produced by Craft Supplies, with the two blanks mounted on the mandrel ready for turning.

honing on a ceramic tile, for an excellent finish and hardly any sanding. Resist any reluctance to turn the barrel down to the correct diameter to match the centre ring. Failure to do this will result in an unattractive pen barrel. Have a few spare tubes and pen blanks to hand, in case you go too far and expose the brass.

11. Burnish with 400-grit or even finer abrasive. Using the versatility of the small variable-speed lathe, reduce the speed for finishing. If sanding and burnishing are carried out at too high a speed, the heat generated can produce fine cracks in the wood. Apply friction polish and follow up with carnauba wax.
12. Lay out the parts of the pen for assembly and follow the instructions provided with the kit. Press the cone into the end of the lower barrel. Push the twist mechanism into the other

Starting to turn down one of the blanks. The fingers of the left hand support the work and the left thumb is held on top of the blade.

The final stages of turning. The diameter must be equal to the diameter of the brass centre ring of the pen.

end of the lower barrel to the line marked on the mechanism itself, and screw the pen refill into the mechanism. Check to see that when twisted clockwise it extends correctly beyond the end of the cone; when twisted anti-clockwise, it should retract into the cone. Fit the pen clip over the end brass fitting, which is pressed in to the top end of the top barrel. Some pens need a small nick filed in the edge of the top rim to give the clip clearance. Slip the brass centre ring over the retracting mechanism and push the top on by hand.

13. Some pen makers like to use adhesive, but the push-fit method should be adequate. Adapt a machine vice (*see* the picture on page 130) to make a relatively cheap pen press, or buy the real thing, which will be more expensive. It is also possible to use a woodworking vice if the jaws open

Check the diameter carefully with Vernier callipers or a micrometer.

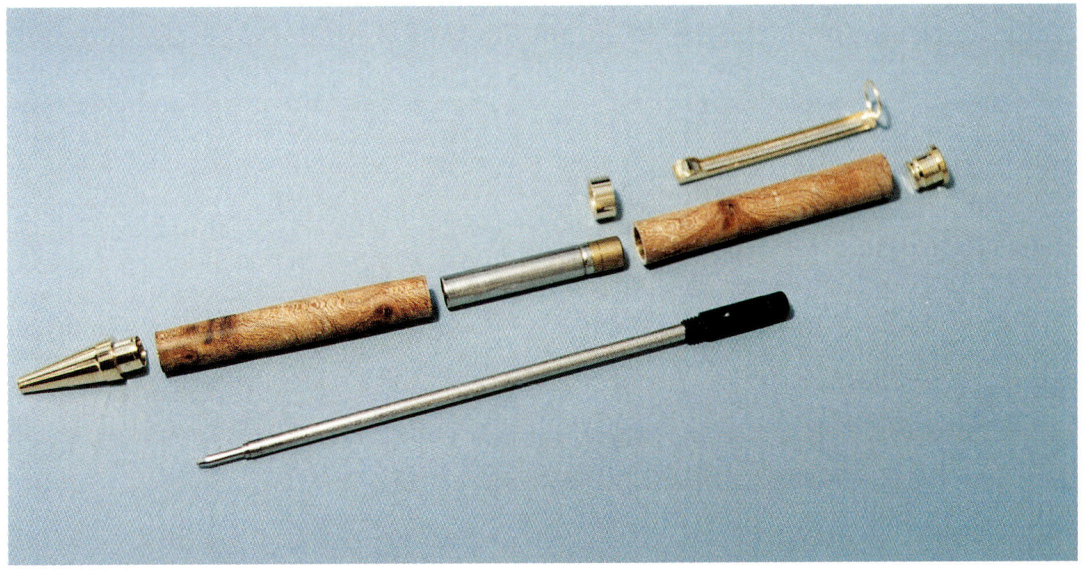

The parts of a pen laid out ready for assembly.

An adapted machine vice makes an effective pen press.

wide enough but wooden or plastic jaws will need to be fitted, to prevent damage to the pen parts. Using a mallet to bang the parts together is asking for trouble!

TURNING A PEN BARREL IN CORIAN

Pen barrels can also be turned from synthetic blanks of materials such as crushed velvet, mother-of-pearl, ivory and reconstituted gemstone, as well as Dymondwood resin-impregnated coloured woods. Corian – a solid plastic used for kitchen worktops and bathroom surrounds – turns extremely well with an oval skew. Offcuts of Corian are often sold at woodworking shows.

The only difference between the process of producing pen barrels from wood and synthetic materials is in the finishing.

1. First cut some 12 × 12 × 150mm blanks with a handsaw and then turn the pen barrels as above. The 12.5mm oval skew works best on materials such as Corian; a gouge and scraper will also do, but the results will not be as good.
2. For the finishing, reduce the lathe speed to 500rpm and sand first with 400-grit abrasive. Follow this by sanding with Micromesh, working through the grades from 1,500 to 12,000. This product is expensive, but it should last up to fifteen times longer than ordinary abrasive because less friction and heat are produced, and the crystals do not become fractured and destroyed. Use the abrasive with a foam block and pass it gently backwards and forwards over the Corian until a scratch-free surface is achieved. If the speed of the lathe is too high, or too much pressure is applied, or both, the friction will generate too much heat. This will result in the Micromesh fusing into the surface of the Corian. A final polish with Brasso or T-Cut (red can) on the lathe, or off the lathe using a polishing mop, will give a superb finish.

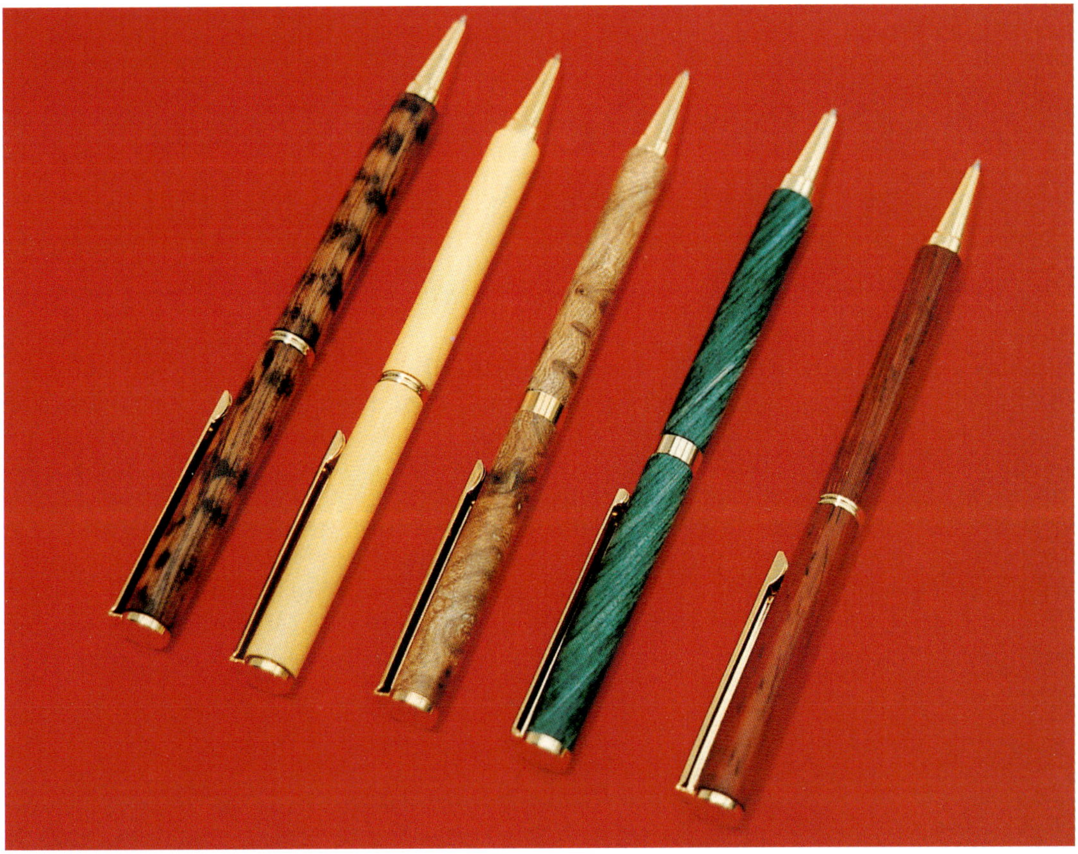

Pens turned in (left to right) snakewood, amarillo, elm burr, Dymondwood and padouk.

Corian produces masses of fine shavings which tend to stick to everything; they are soon vacuumed up.

— 13 —

INTRODUCTION TO LACE BOBBIN TURNING

Lace bobbin turning is very popular and a craft in its own right. The little spindles are great fun to turn, and present a good way to practise between-centre turning. There are many types of bobbin and many complex designs. When making bobbins that are actually going to be used for lacemaking, consult with the intended user first because preferences in shape and proportion vary from one lacemaker to another.

Lace bobbins require very little wood. Blanks in all sorts of exotic timbers can be purchased already cut square, and to the right dimension, ready to put straight on the lathe. The equipment is simple; the MT shank of a lace bobbin drive can be inserted into the headstock spindle or alternatively into the quick-release carrier for the micro chuck. The second method is necessary for indexing and decorating the body of the bobbin if the lathe does

Selection of lace bobbins.

not have an indexing facility. For elaborate decoration it is important to be able to lock the lathe while working.

There is tremendous scope for decoration. A flexible drive will take a number of different-shaped cutters and burrs to produce texture and indentations. The tail of the bobbin is usually drilled to take a hoop of wire with glass beads, called a 'spangle'. Coloured woods can be mixed to achieve contrast, or wood can be combined with inserts of turned polyester resin. Some bobbins are spiralled and fine wire is added.

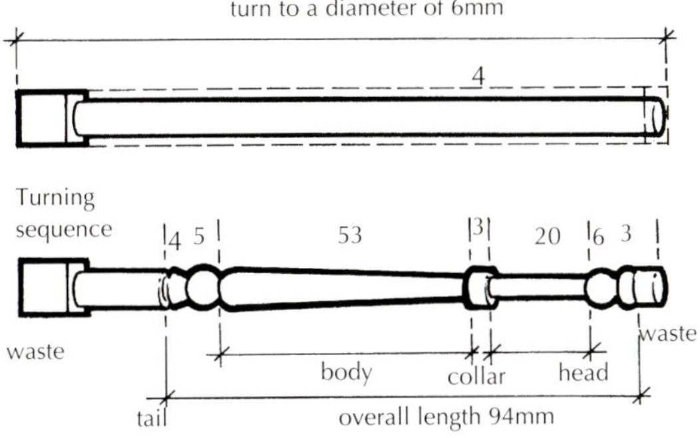

A simple East Midlands lace bobbin.

TURNING AN EAST MIDLANDS LACE BOBBIN

1. Start with an accurately prepared blank 127mm long × 9 × 9mm. Mark the centre at one end and centre pop so that the revolving centre can give tailstock support.
2. Place a lace bobbin drive in the headstock and a revolving centre in the tailstock, and mount the work. Set the lathe speed to 2,000rpm and position the toolrest.
3. Turn the blank to the round using a skew chisel to produce a uniform cylinder with a diameter of 6mm. Take time and, as the work becomes round, support the spindle with the forefinger of the left hand.
4. With the lathe rotating, shade in with pencil 6mm at the tailstock end; this will be waste wood. Mark in the lengths and diameters of the head and tail of the bobbin (*see* the picture on page 135), taking the measurements from the edge of the waste wood.
5. Follow the sequence (*see* the picture on

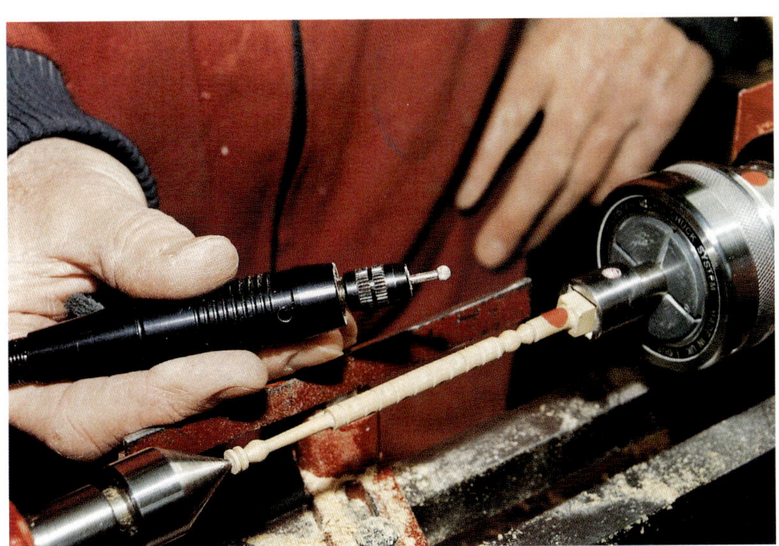

Partly turned bobbin about to be indented for decoration, with a round-ended diamond burr held in a flexible drive. The lathe being used does not have a built-in indexing facility so the lace bobbin drive is held in the carrier in the Micro chuck, which has indexing; the chuck body can be firmly locked by means of the index bar.

Acrylic paint is applied to decorative indentations with a fine brush. When the paint is dry, a quick spin and a touch of fine abrasive will remove any that has spread, so that the indentations have good clean edges.

A turned Corian insert being glued into a boxwood bobbin to decorate the body. The Corian has been drilled 3mm right through and is secured to the bobbin by means of a spigot and superglue. Effective contrasts can be created by mixing wood with alternative materials such as cast polyester resin.

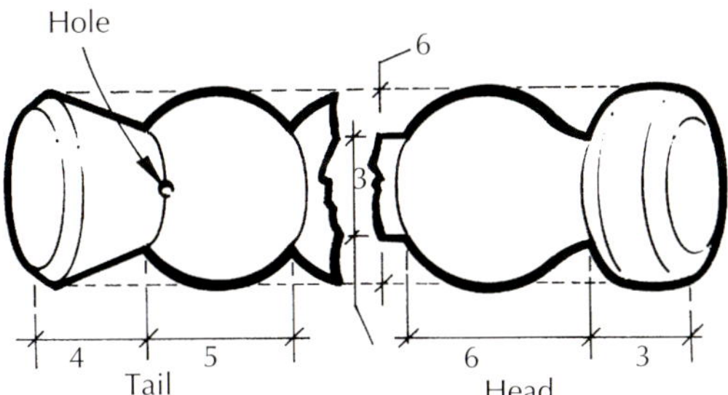

The head and tail of an East Midlands lace bobbin.

Using a turning guide to mark out the blank (coloured red), which has already been turned to the round. With the lathe revolving at slow speed, a pencil is held against the guide to mark the lines.

Turning the tail of the bobbin with a 12.5mm oval skew. The fingers need to be very close to the end of the tool and the work, but the traces of red are paint, not blood! The lace bobbin drive is inserted directly into the headstock with a thread protector.

page 133), taking gentle cuts and giving finger support to the spindle. Novices will break a few lace bobbins but, with practice and concentration, a bobbin will be produced that needs little or no sanding.

6. Part off the waste wood at the head and tail. Use the long point of a skew first, then stop the lathe and complete the parting off by hand with a fine saw. Hand sand the cut ends to make them smooth.

— 14 —

TURNING FOR THE DOLLS' HOUSE

Collecting and displaying $\frac{1}{12}$in- or even $\frac{1}{24}$in-scale furniture and equipment in a dolls' house is a fascinating hobby. With patience and practice, many tiny items can be turned for the house, from table tops right down to knobs for a chest of drawers! Miniature lathes offer the opportunity to make items in this scale.

The instructions below describe how to make a basic table leg (*see also* page 86), using tools and equipment that are better suited to such small work. The techniques can be applied to most miniature spindle work for the dolls' house, including stair balusters, newel posts, chair legs, lamps, four-poster bed posts, and so on. Turning a set of matching spindles needs planning and concentration.

Although dolls'-house hobbyists use the imperial scale – $\frac{1}{12}$in – dimensions given are given here in millimetres. A rough rule of thumb when working in this scale is 2mm = 1 inch.

MATERIALS

Use fine-grain wood for miniature scale work. If the item is to be painted this is not

Two pedestal tables, one with a tilting top. The table tops were turned using the pressure-pad method and the pedestals were turned between centres. One table (left) is stained to represent mahogany and the other (right) is made from pearwood, with a very distinctive, if slightly out of scale, grain.

Dolls' house chest of drawers made in pearwood and sycamore with turned pearwood knobs.

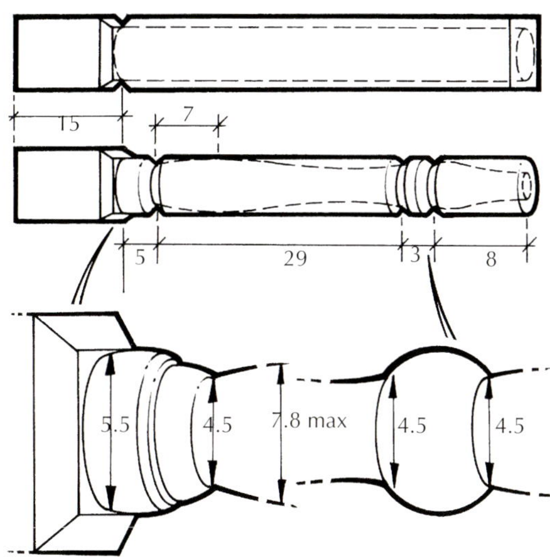

A 1/12in scale table leg.

so critical. Sometimes it is better to stain wood after turning to represent the wood required rather than to use the real thing. For example, the table leg described below is intended for a pine country-style kitchen table, but using real pine would be wrong and sycamore has been used instead. Woods such as lemonwood, boxwood, sycamore, pear, holly or antique reclaimed mahogany are all suitable for modelling; they all polish, stain or paint well.

TURNING A 1/12IN-SCALE TABLE LEG

Equipment	Micro chuck, quick-release carrier, lace bobbin drive, revolving centre
Turning tools	Miniature turning tools
Materials	Four blanks of 8 × 8 × 60mm fine-grain hardwood

This design represents a full-sized leg 710mm long turned from 100 × 100mm timber. Before turning a spindle it is important to plan exactly how the shape is to be achieved, and plot the position of the initial cuts and the maximum and minimum diameters. These measurements can be transferred to a piece of card to give guide lines (*see* the picture above). This helps in making more than one of the same item over and over again.

1. Cut four blanks 8 × 8 × 60mm long from carefully prepared wood, planed all round, so that they are absolutely square in cross section, and centre pop one end. Insert the lace bobbin drive into the micro chuck fitted with the 1MT tool carrier or directly into the headstock spindle. Place a small revolving centre in the tailstock. The short toolrest is used so that it can be positioned as close to the work as possible.
2. Place the end of the spindle blank in the lace bobbin drive and apply gentle pressure at the tailstock end. Too much pressure will result in the square edges

at the top of the spindle being rounded and a thin spindle will bow in the centre.

3. Set the lathe speed to 3,000rpm. (Remember the general rule: the smaller the diameter of the work, the faster the lathe speed.)
4. Using the card turning guide, with the datum lines clearly shown, mark with a pencil the position of the first V cut at the headstock end of the spindle. Note that the wood in the lace bobbin drive, and up to the first V cut, will remain square. Take a 12.5mm oval skew and with the long point make a V cut at the pencil line.
5. Using the same skew, turn the section between the V cut and the tailstock to a diameter of a little over 7.8mm.
6. With the turning guide as an aid, mark the remaining three Vs in pencil and then make the cuts with an oval skew.
7. Form the curved section at the middle of the leg with an oval skew, always cutting downhill.
8. Form the foot with the micro oval skew, always cutting downhill, keeping the bevel close to the wood and, as the end of the cut is approached, moving to the short point of the tool.
9. Turn the bead at the bottom of the leg, making sure that the top is well rounded. Turn another bead at the top of the leg in a similar manner and then turn a small fillet to add detail.
10. Only sand the spindle if it is really necessary; sanding too vigorously will reduce the crispness of the turning and lose detail. It is not really possible to friction polish the leg in the lathe because of the square top. In any case, the whole piece of furniture may require staining before polishing and this is best done in one operation.
11. Repeat the turning process for the remaining legs.

A 1/12in scale Victorian kitchen table with four turned legs.

TURNING A 1/12IN-SCALE CANDLESTICK

Equipment	Micro chuck, quick-release tool carrier, 6mm two-prong drive, small drill chuck, revolving centre
Turning tools	Micro gouges and chisels
Materials	15mm × 15mm × 50mm fine-grain hardwood

This project involves techniques for very small faceplate work, which can be applied to many other similar items. The chucking methods used ensure that expensive wood is not wasted. Most of the work can be carried out with the micro spindle gouge and the micro oval skew and with the lathe speed set at 3,000rpm. Support the back of the work with a forefinger and use the thumb of the left hand to steady the tool on the toolrest. The right hand is interlocked with the left hand, rather like a golf grip, to control the micro chisels.

Note: in some pictures, the hands have been moved back to show the work and the tool clearly.

1. Centre pop both ends of a blank of fine-grain hardwood 15 × 15 × 50mm long. Insert a 6mm two-prong drive into the chuck fitted with the tool carrier or insert the drive directly into the headstock. Fit a small revolving centre in the tailstock.
2. Mount the blank between centres and turn a cylinder using a small gouge. Form a 20mm long × 6mm diameter spigot at the tailstock end with the parting tool. Remove the work from the lathe.
3. Remove the tailstock and replace the two-prong drive with a small drill chuck. Mount the blank with the spigot in the drill chuck and tighten.
4. First turn the candle, 10mm long × 2mm diameter, with a micro gouge and a micro skew. Form a very small spigot to represent the wick with a micro parting tool.
5. Working from the end of the candle, towards the headstock, develop the shape of the candlestick. The maximum diameter of the stem is 4mm and the minimum, just above the base, is 3mm.
6. Burnishing with non-woven web should be all that is necessary. Begin parting off with the micro parting tool and aim to produce a slightly concave underside but leave a small spigot. Switch off the lathe and cut through the remaining wood with a fine saw.
7. Paint the candle with white acrylic paint and dab the wick with a black felt pen.

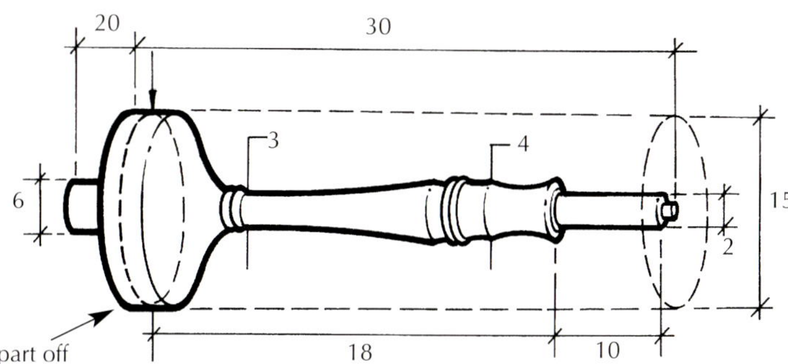

Candlestick in 1/12 scale.

Candlesticks and other tiny items to go in the dolls' house.

TURNING 1/12IN ITEMS FOR THE DOLLS'-HOUSE GARDEN

Equipment	50mm faceplate
Turning tools	Miniature and micro gouges and chisels
Materials	Suitable blanks in fine-grain hardwood

When turning items for the garden of the dolls' house, scale is not critical, but some dimensions are given here for guidance. Seek inspiration in gardens that are open to the public, or at garden centres. Start with terracotta flowerpots and progress (in order of difficulty) to the birdbath, planters and pedestal.

All these examples are turned with the blank glued to a glue chuck held on a faceplate. This is an efficient, safe and inexpensive way of holding wood for turning; it leaves no holes in the work, there are no chuck jaws whirring round to catch unwary fingers and very little wood is wasted. A small faceplate will be needed.

1. If matching pairs are planned, make a turning guide first, to ensure the same dimensions in both.
2. To produce a flowerpot, prepare a blank of fine-grain wood to the dimensions (*see* the picture on page 141) and hot-melt glue the blank to a glue chuck held on a faceplate in the headstock of the lathe. Set the lathe speed to 2,000rpm throughout turning, but drop the speed to 1,500 for sanding and burnishing so that the friction created will not scorch the wood.
3. In each case, turn the blank to the round first and then face off the end

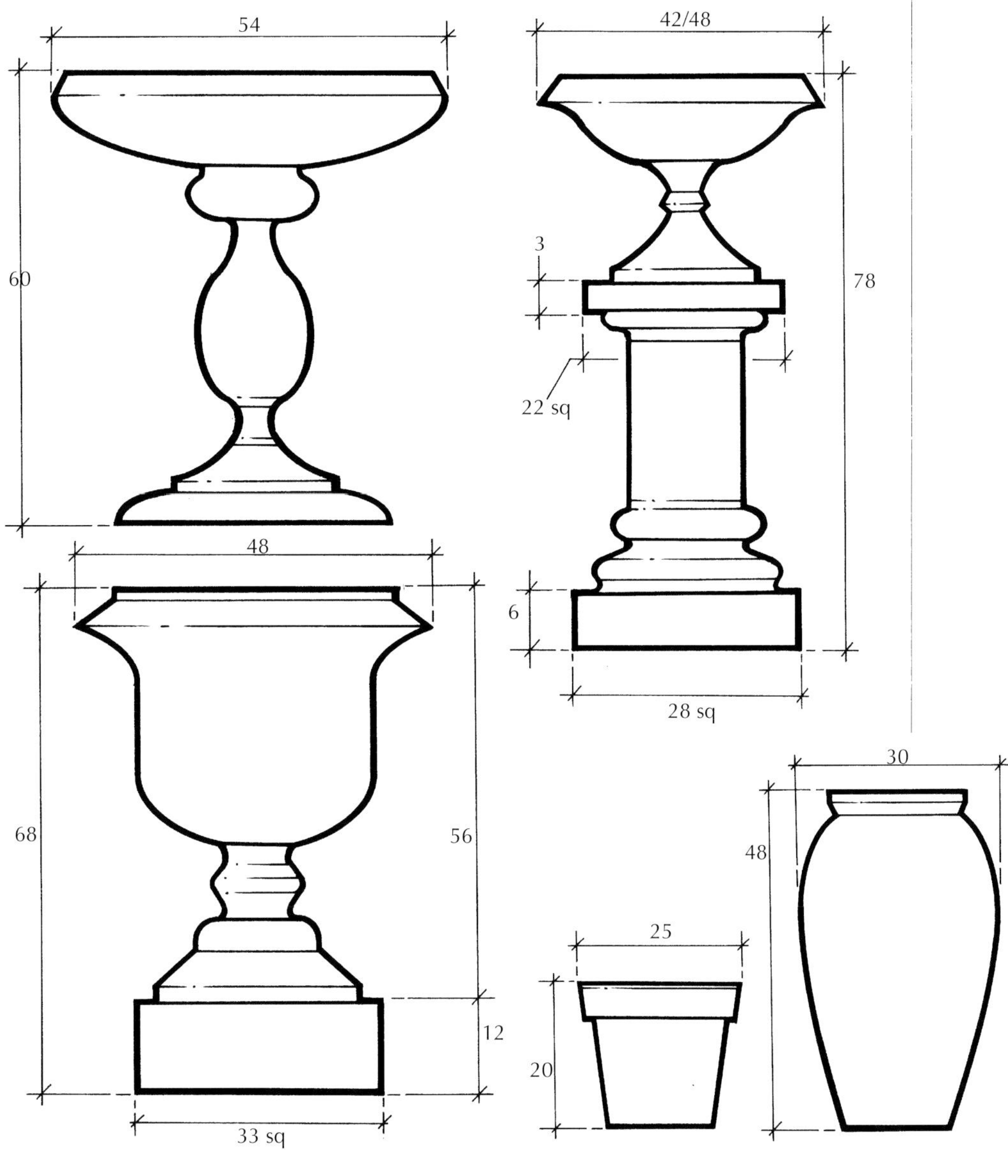

Garden containers and birdbath all in ½in scale.

using a 6mm spindle gouge. Where applicable, hollow out the end of the blank to the desired shape using a 6mm miniature or a 4mm micro gouge. The birdbath and the planter on the pedestal have quite shallow dishes. In the case of the flowerpots, the deep planter and the Ali Baba pot, use a 4mm beading tool because the holes are deeper and more wood needs to be removed. Use the end gauge of the callipers to check depth.

4. Remove the toolrest. Sand and burnish the area that has been hollowed out.
5. Replace the toolrest and mark on the wood any helpful lines to guide the

Little terracotta flowerpots can be turned in different sizes. A drainage hole in the bottom makes them look even more authentic.

Partially parting through the base of a shallow planter with a thin parting tool. Using this tool, very little wood is wasted.

formation of the outer shape. Starting outboard, develop the outer shape with a small spindle gouge and make final, detailed cuts with a skew. Always cut downhill and keep the bevel as close to the wood as possible to give the smoothest cut. Stop to hone tools at regular intervals to keep them really sharp.

6. Take measurements, both diameter and length, off the drawing with callipers and apply them to the wood at each stage – with the lathe *stationary*.
7. Remove the toolrest, sand with 400-grit abrasive and burnish with ultra-fine non-woven web abrasive.
8. Use a thin parting tool and part off until 4mm of wood is left, slightly undercutting. Cut through the remaining wood with a fine-toothed saw and with the lathe stationary. (With more experience, these small items can be parted off completely, although there is always a risk that the part will fly off and get lost in the shavings!)

The pedestal for the planter is more challenging. Mark the main positions where beads and fillets are to be cut and using a skew and spindle gouge develop the middle section of the parallel column. With a 4mm micro gouge develop the cove at the base and the two beads and finally the top bead. Use a 4mm beading tool to turn the two small fillets on either side of the cove at the base and the fillets at the top and bottom of the parallel part of the column. These fillets give the turning a crisp appearance. The square plinths at the top and bottom are cut and glued in position; take care to line them up accurately.

A deep planter on a plinth, a sundial, an Ali Baba pot and a flowerpot, all turned in sycamore. Acrylic paints are used to paint the wood to represent stone or terracotta.

TINY SAUCEPAN WITH LID AND HANDLE

Equipment	Micro chuck, MJ35 jaws, SCO4 screwchuck, quick-release carrier, small drill chuck
Turning tools	Miniature and micro gouges and chisels
Materials	Very fine-grain hardwood such as boxwood; 24mm diameter × 30mm for pot; 4mm × 4mm × 35mm for handle

As items decrease in diameter, it becomes more comfortable to use the micro chuck with the MJ35 accessory jaws for faceplate turning. The smaller jaws do not protrude beyond the diameter of the screwchuck insert and this makes them safer to use when working close to the turning wood. The technique used is still the glue chucking method. If a micro chuck is not available, simply use the smallest faceplate possible and taper the end of the glue chuck to reduce the diameter of the outside face; this will stop it getting in the way.

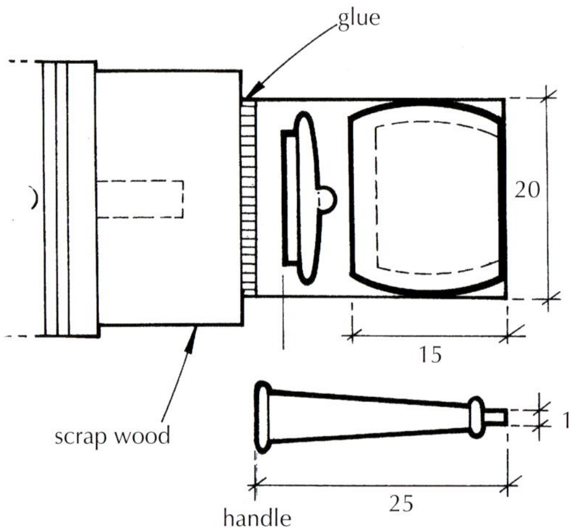

A 1/12in scale saucepan.

1. Make a glue chuck from scrap wood and screw it on to the SCO4 screwchuck insert placed in the MJ35 jaws. Face off the end. Select a piece of boxwood branch 24mm diameter × 30mm long and glue to the glue chuck.
2. Turn the blank with a small gouge to a diameter of 20mm and use a 4mm micro spindle gouge to form the outer shape of the saucepan to a length of 15mm.
3. Hollow out the inside of the saucepan with the micro parting tool and the scraper. Tidy up the inner bottom surface with the square end of the scraper.
4. Begin parting off, making sure that the bottom surface is slightly concave, and leaving a small spigot. Stop the lathe and cut through the spigot with a fine saw.
5. Form the lid and its knob from the remaining wood on the glue chuck. Set the callipers to the inside top diameter of the saucepan and use the parting tool to form a matching lip, so that the lid fits snugly. Then part off as before.
6. Replace the screwchuck and jaws with the quick-release carrier and a small drill chuck and form the handle by taking a piece of wood 4 × 4 × 35mm, paring off one end and inserting it into a drill chuck. Turn a handle 25mm long with a 1mm spigot on the end.
7. Drill a small hole in the saucepan and glue in the handle spigot. Paint the saucepan and lid inside and outside with black acrylic paint to give a convincing matt iron appearance, white inside and a colour outside to simulate an enamelled saucepan, or use aluminium paint for a modern pan.

Smaller saucepans, frying pans and even a kettle can be made in a similar way.

Turned saucepans, warming pan, milk churn and chimney pots, all in 1/12in scale.

TURNING TINY PLATTERS AND BOWLS

Equipment	Micro chuck, MJ35 jaws, SCO4 screwchuck
Turning tools	Miniature and micro gouges and chisels
Materials	Very fine-grain hardwood such as boxwood; 24mm diameter × 30mm

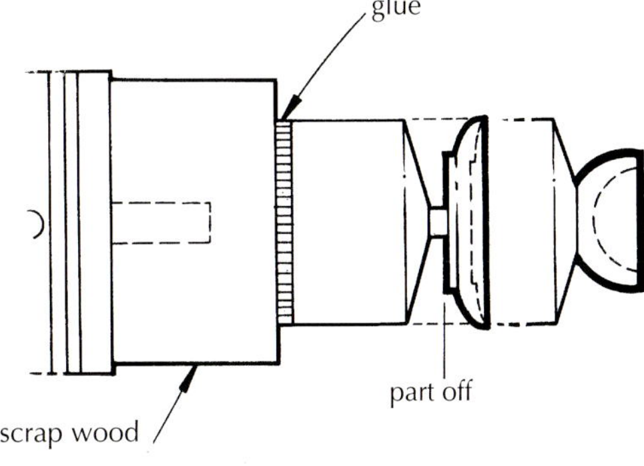

Platters and bowls in 1/12in scale.

1. Use the same combination of chuck jaws, screwchuck and glue chuck as for the tiny saucepan. Hot-melt glue a piece of boxwood 24mm diameter × 30mm thick to the glue chuck. Because boxwood has a very fine grain, an excellent finish can be achieved straight from the scraper or parting tool; this is not possible with coarse-grained woods.

2. Turn the blank to 20mm diameter using a small gouge and form a dished top surface for the platter with a 4mm micro spindle gouge, making sure that there is no centre mark left. Using a micro parting tool, remove sufficient wood to enable the underside of the rim to be formed and then continue to cut the bottom surface slightly concave. Aim to produce as thin a section as possible.

3. Part until a small spigot is left, which can be cut with a saw when the lathe is stationary. Further platters can be made using the remaining wood on the chuck.

All sorts of bowls and trays can be turned in a similar way.

Wooden bowls, platters and vases turned in boxwood.

SPECIAL EFFECTS

The wood of items turned for the dolls' house can be finished to represent other materials, such as china, terracotta, copper, stone, brass or galvanized metal. The process is fairly lengthy for such small items, but those who work in $\frac{1}{12}$in scale are not usually short of patience!

To simulate china, apply a coat of white acrylic paint while the bowl is still held on the lathe. When the paint is dry, spin the bowl and use a very fine abrasive to sand almost back to the wood. Repeat this several times to achieve a very fine finish. Burnishing with non-woven nylon web will give an almost translucent effect, and the abrasive can be simply washed out and used again and again when it becomes clogged with paint. To finish, paint the rim of the bowl in a contrasting colour with the lathe slowly rotating.

To achieve a galvanized iron finish for a milk churn, for example, apply a base coat of acrylic silver and then build up several coats as above. A coat of pewter paste

Acrylic paints, gold, stone and metal finishes.

Doll's house table, the top, frame and legs all turned, as well as all the other items, including the lampshade and the napkin ring. The decanter is turned from clear acrylic and the planter has been painted with acrylics.

applied with a cloth to the rotating wood over the paint will give the desired effect. When dry, add a little extra touch by applying bronze or copper paste to represent bands on the churn as the work rotates.

To give a worn appearance, a metal object can be painted first with copper and then with a coat of silver. When dry, gently rub off some of the silver to reveal the copper.

All these methods will tie up the lathe for some time, so have a few spare faceplates to interchange while the paint dries.

— 15 —

SHIP MODELLING TECHNIQUES

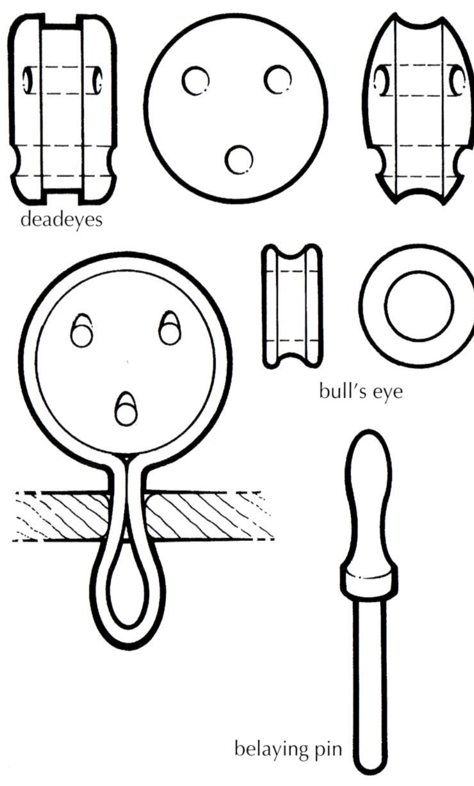

Turned items to be found on a ship model.

Many items on this model ship were turned.

It is immensely satisfying for modellers of period ships to make all the ship's parts, from the smallest deadeye to the ropes and rigging, by hand, and as near to museum standard as possible. Although it is possible to turn very small items on a full-sized lathe, miniature metal-turning and woodturning lathes are perfect for this type of work. They offer a high top speed and all-round access, are quieter to use over long periods, and the best offer all the precision required.

The techniques involved in turning really small items may be applied to the production of any round parts required for modelling, from pieces for aircraft and railway layouts to bits for vehicles and carts. In this context, 'small' means 'very small indeed', but the point is not 'how tiny?' but 'how accurate?' This type of turning is not artistic; it is, in effect, model engineering in wood. Many modellers do not produce the whole model, but instead show off their work in a small display or diorama.

SCALE

The aim is to make a scaled-down replica of each item found on a model and scale is all-important. Most model ships on display in museums are 1:48 scale, which means that 1in scale = 48in in real size, or 12in (1ft) = ¼in (6.35mm). When researching a ship to model, all the dimensions on original plans will be in feet and inches. Converting all the dimensions into metric measurement makes them easier to use and work with. The 1:48 scale is used here as a baseline, and it is not difficult to scale up or down as required.

Actual size in inches	1:48 scale in mm
1	0.53
2	1.06
3	1.59
4	2.12
5	2.65
6	3.18
7	3.71
8	4.24
9	4.77
10	5.30
11	5.83
12	6.35

MATERIALS

Although the ships themselves were built in oak, teak and pine, these timbers are not suitable for a model because the relatively coarse grain will look out of place. Contemporary model ships were traditionally made in boxwood, ebony, ivory and bone. Fine-grain hardwoods can be stained, painted or coloured to represent other woods and metals. For more detailed information on this, *see* Chapter 5.

ITEMS FOR SHIP MODELS

The following items are to be found on many ship models. All the examples highlight various useful turning techniques.

BELAYING PINS

Equipment	Micro chuck, MJ15 jaws, micro tools
Materials	6.4 × 6.4 × 50mm boxwood

Belaying pins are used for securing ropes on the ship and are usually positioned in a rack. They are created by turning the smallest of spindles.

A 6.4 × 6.4 × 50mm long boxwood blank is held in compression mode in the MJ15 jaws, fitted in the micro chuck. Hold 20mm of the blank in the chuck with 30mm projecting; no tailstock support is necessary. The blank is turned using a micro oval skew to the desired shape (*see* the picture on page 148). During the turning the left-hand forefinger supports the spindle.

With the lathe running at 4,000rpm, the turning is begun on the parallel part of the pin and then the handle is shaped. Gently part the pin off with the long point of an oval skew. The finish should be so good that no sanding will be needed.

It may seem a waste of wood to start with such a large blank, but this gives sufficient rigidity and ensures that there is no chatter.

PILLARS

Equipment	Micro chuck, quick-release carrier, revolving centre, modified Marlin point, micro turning tools
Materials	Boxwood in blank sizes as required

Pillars are required in various parts of a ship. Use a Swiss file and adapt a Marlin point to produce a small friction drive 2mm diameter × 8mm long; spare points can be purchased and they are relatively inexpensive.

To turn a pillar, cut the blank to the required length and drill the ends with a 2mm diameter drill. Dowels can later be inserted into these holes as a method of securing the pillar to the rails and deck. Mount the blank between centres with the improvised pin in the headstock and a revolving centre in the tailstock. Turn to shape with the micro gouge and skew.

Making more than one pillar of the same shape, requires practice and is always a challenge. Start with carefully prepared blanks and a simple turning guide to make the task easier. Make a few extra pillars; be critical and throw away those that are not up to standard. Remember, 'near enough' is not 'good enough'.

BLOCKS

Equipment	Micro chuck, MJ15 jaws, revolving centre, Marlin collet chuck and fine twist drill, micro turning tools
Materials	Boxwood in blank sizes as required

Blocks have pulleys or sheaves fitted inside the block and rotate on a pin. The diameters of these sheaves, and their drilled holes, will vary considerably, depending on the size of the block. For the larger sheaves, which work well in ebony, the MJ20 chuck jaws may be more appropriate.

Hold the blank in the MJ15 jaws in compression mode and turn to the required diameter. Face off with the long point of a micro oval skew and then cut a groove for the rope with the smallest gouge. Hold the Marlin collet chuck in the tailstock, fitted with a collet suitable for the fine twist drill selected, and drill the central hole. Part off and repeat the process with the remaining wood to produce as many sheaves of the same size as required.

DEADEYES

Equipment	Micro chuck, MJ15 jaws, revolving centre, micro turning tools
Materials	Boxwood in blank sizes as required

Deadeyes of differing sizes are used on a real ship to tension the shrouds by means of lanyards. They consist of a round wooden block with convex outer surfaces, a central groove for the shroud and three holes equally spaced through which the lanyards are passed (*see* the picture on page 148). The correct dimensions for all these fittings are carefully and precisely documented and can be found in the many books written on rigging merchant and naval ships.

The method of turning is similar to that described for the sheave except that the deadeyes are fatter and the outer surface is convex. The three holes are drilled off the lathe.

GUN BARRELS

Equipment	Micro chuck, MJ15 or MJ20 jaws, drill chuck, revolving centre, micro turning tools
Materials	Fine-grain wood in blank sizes as required

Turning up different-sized gun barrels in ebony or boxwood is great fun. Most guns

Very small holes being drilled in turned model ship deadeyes, held in a jig secured in a machine vice. The small, well-engineered 85w Proxxon bench drill will take either a drill chuck or a collet chuck. It is extremely accurate with three high-precision bearings and three speeds – 1,800, 4,700 and 8,500rpm. The drill has a quill travel of 30mm and a throat depth of 140mm. Deadeyes of differing sizes are shown in the foreground. A small pillar drill, together with a good-quality machine vice, help the modeller to achieve the best possible results.

are cast iron and black, so ebony is a good wood to use; as an alternative, boxwood can be stained or painted with matt black or finished with a metallic paint to produce a bronzed look.

Prepare a blank of the correct size and find a twist drill of the right diameter for the gun bore. Choose a set of jaws to use in the micro chuck to suit the size of the blank and bring up the tailstock to give support. Turn the wood to the round. Replace the revolving centre with a drill chuck with a 1MT shank and drill the muzzle end of the barrel. Replace the revolving centre and turn to shape with the micro oval skew.

ANYTHING ELSE?

Buckets, pumps, lamps, binnacles, wooden mast hoops, barrels, chimneys, vents, portholes, fenders and lifebelts can all be turned and added to models. The Multistar micro chuck with its small jaws, together with the Marlin system and its accessories, gives the turner a choice of ways to hold very small blanks for turning.

INDEXED ITEMS

To turn indexed fittings such as capstans, windlasses and ship's wheels exactly to scale demands a great deal of patience and skill. Some modellers will be quite content with a representative item, on which some of the detail has been simplified. For example, the holes in a capstan to take the bars should be square, not round. To overcome this problem, drill the holes on the lathe using the indexing facility for spacing and then, with the aid of a square Swiss file, square off the entrance to the hole to give the impression that the hole is square throughout. This method can also be applied to the barrel of the windlass.

Some fittings are actually made up of a number of different pieces of wood but the modeller will probably turn one piece of wood and use a file, or plane, to produce flats where appropriate.

Ship's wheels are particularly complex and making a precise model will involve a good deal of work. The section of the spoke that goes through the rim should really be square, but an effective wheel can be made with a completely round

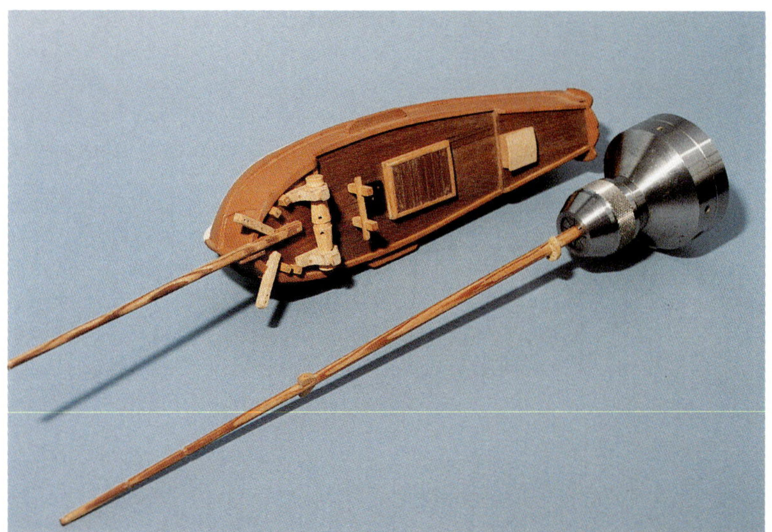

The APTC collet chuck holding the main mast for a small model ship.

A model of a ship's carronade, in a larger scale, showing in detail the gun barrel, cannonball, rammer and sponge, which were all turned in sycamore and then painted.

spoke passing through a correspondingly round hole in the rim. The spaces between the holes are achieved using the indexing on the lathe or chuck, but this can be problematic if there are ten spokes, for example – which often seems to be the case! To make an absolutely exact replica, a manual method for indexing will need to be applied (*see* Chapter 7 on drilling and indexing).

MASTS, SPARS, BOWSPRITS AND JIBBOOMS

Equipment	Micro chuck, MJ15 jaws, revolving centre
Materials	Boxwood in blank sizes as required

When creating these items, the lathe is used purely as a sanding machine. Some of the spars will be very small in diameter but quite long. Some sections of a spar or mast are square or octagonal, and they are often tapered, so an element of woodworking, using conventional tools off the lathe, will be necessary first. The partly fashioned spar can then be secured in the chuck jaws and sanded to its final shape with fine abrasive. Often this operation has to be carried out without tailstock support and with the fingers acting as a steady. If the lathe has a hollow headstock the spar can be passed right through the headstock and the ends shaped, with only a short amount extending beyond the jaws.

If the turner cannot devise a method of spinning a mast or spar in the lathe, there is always the alternative of making it in parts and joining it together; after all, this is how many full-sized masts or spars were constructed in reality.

Modelling, and turning in general, requires a certain amount of ingenuity and it is the constant challenges that make this type of work so enjoyable. The satisfaction comes from solving a problem and having admirers ask, ‘How on earth did you do that?’

Always persevere and finish a model, even if some of the detail is not as precise or as accurate as you would like; an unfinished, discarded model can only be described as a failure. Set an objective, or a number of objectives, for the next project, to achieve constant improvement in skill and standard.

SUPPLIERS

The products mentioned in this book are available from the following suppliers, many of whom have comprehensive catalogues.

APTC
Tel: 0800 371822
Carbatec MkII
Ian Wilkie friction drive
Junior collet chuck
50mm diameter faceplates
Hot-melt glue sticks
Cast polyester resin

Ashley Iles
Tel: 01790 763372
Miniature turning tools

Brimarc
Tel: 01926 493389
Proxxon range of miniature machines

Chesterman
Tel: 01785 503345
Ceramic tiles
Spring clamps

Craft Supplies
Tel: 0800 146417
Mini-Grip 1000 chuck
Miniature turning tools
Woodturning accessories
Wood
Lace bobbin blanks
Cast polyester resin
Ian Wilkie artificial ivory and boxwood tool
Micromesh abrasive
Supplies for pen making

Crown
Tel: 0114 2723366
Miniature turning tools
Micro turning tools
Thin parting tool
Armrest

CSM Just Abrasives
Tel: 01273 600434
Webrax
Hermes J-flex abrasive
Carrol Sanders

Emco
Tel: 01780 740956
Unimat lathe

Henry Taylor
Tel: 0114 2340282
Miniature turning tools
Thin parting tool

Peter Child
Tel: 01787 237291
Screwchuck
Woodturning accessories

Planet
Tel: 01686 626260
Slimline revolving centre
Pen mandrel

Rexon
Tel: 01709 361158
WL618A Miniature lathe

Selbix
Tel: 01376 550552
Mini lathe
Mini chuck

Tecmark
Tel: 01223 422160
Moldex disposable masks

Trend
Tel: 01923 224657
Airshield helmet

Turners Retreat
Tel: 01302 744344
Miniature turning tools
Wood and woodturning accessories
Drilling jig
Supplies for pen making

Whilst this book was in production Multistar unfortunately went into voluntary liquidation. Readers may therefore have difficulty in obtaining the Micro chuck. The Selbix Mini chuck is recommended as a suitable alternative. It has three sets of jaws and is an excellent and very safe chuck to use.

IMPERIAL TO METRIC CONVERSION TABLE

Inch	0	1	2	3	4	5	6	7	8
0	0.00	25.40	50.80	76.20	101.60	127.00	152.40	177.80	203.20
1/64	0.40	25.80	51.20	76.60	102.00	127.40	152.80	178.20	203.60
1/32	0.79	26.19	51.59	76.99	102.39	127.79	153.19	178.59	203.99
1/16	1.59	26.99	52.39	77.79	103.19	128.59	153.99	179.39	204.79
5/64	1.98	27.38	52.79	78.18	103.58	129.98	154.38	189.78	205.18
3/32	2.38	27.78	53.18	78.58	103.98	129.38	154.78	180.18	205.58
7/64	2.78	28.18	53.58	78.98	104.38	129.78	155.18	180.58	205.98
1/8	3.18	28.58	53.98	79.38	104.78	130.18	155.58	180.98	206.38
9/64	3.57	28.97	54.37	79.77	105.17	130.57	155.97	181.37	206.77
5/32	3,97	29.37	54.77	80.17	105.57	130.97	156.37	181.77	207.17
11/64	4.37	39.77	55.17	80.57	105.97	131.37	156.77	182.17	207.15
3/16	4.76	30.16	55.56	80.96	106.36	131.76	157.16	182.56	207.96
13/64	5.16	30.56	55.96	81.35	106.76	132.16	157.56	182.96	208.36
7/32	5.56	30.96	56.36	81.76	107.16	132.56	157.96	183.36	208.76
15/64	5.95	31.35	56.75	82.15	107.55	132.95	158.35	183.75	209.15
1/4	6.35	31.75	57.15	82.55	107.95	133.35	158.75	184.15	209.55
17/64	6.75	32.15	57.55	82.94	108.35	133.75	159.15	184.55	209.95
9/32	7.14	32.54	57.94	83.34	108.74	134.14	159.54	184.94	210.34
19/64	7.54	32.94	58.34	83.74	109.14	134.54	159.94	185.34	210.74
5/16	7.94	33.34	58.74	84.14	109.54	134.94	160.34	185.74	211.14
21/64	8.33	33.73	59.13	84.53	109.93	135.33	160.73	186.13	211.53
11/32	8.73	34.13	59.53	84.93	110.33	135.73	161.13	186.56	211.93
23/64	9.13	34.53	59.93	85.33	110.73	136.13	161.53	186.93	212.33
3/8	9.53	34.93	60.33	85.73	111.13	136.53	161.93	187.33	212.73
25/64	9.92	35.32	60.72	86.12	111.52	136.92	162.32	187.72	213.12
13/32	10.32	35.72	61.12	86.52	111.92	137.32	162.72	188.12	213.52
27/64	10.72	36.12	61.52	86.92	112.32	137.72	163.12	188.52	213.92
7/16	11.11	36.51	61.91	87.31	112.71	138.11	163.51	188.91	214.31
26/64	11.51	36.91	62.31	87.71	113.11	138.51	163.91	189.31	214.71
15/32	11.91	37.31	62.71	88.11	113.51	138.91	164.31	189.71	215.11
31/64	12.30	37.70	63.10	88.50	113.90	139.30	164.70	190.10	215.50
1/2	12.70	38.10	63.50	88.90	114.30	139.70	165.10	190.50	215.90

Inch	0	1	2	3	4	5	6	7	8
33/64	13.10	38.50	63.90	89.30	114.70	140.10	165.50	190.90	216.30
17/32	13.49	38.89	64.29	89.69	115.09	140.49	165.89	191.29	216.69
35/64	13.89	39.29	64.69	90.09	115.49	140.89	166.29	191.69	217.09
9/16	14.29	39.69	65.09	90.88	111.28	141.29	166.69	192.09	217.49
37/64	14.68	40.08	65.48	90.88	116.28	141.68	167.08	192.48	217.88
19/32	15.08	40.48	65.88	91.28	116.68	142.08	167.48	192.88	218.28
39/64	15.48	40.88	66.28	91.68	117.08	142.48	167.88	193.28	218.68
5/8	15.88	41.28	66.68	92.08	117.48	142.88	168.28	193.68	219.08
41/64	16.27	41.67	67.07	92.47	117.87	143.27	168.67	194.07	219.47
21/32	16.67	42.07	67.47	92.87	118.27	143.67	169.07	194.47	219.87
43/64	17.07	42.47	67.87	93.27	118.67	144.07	169.47	194.87	220.27
11/16	17.46	42.86	68.26	93.66	119.06	144.46	169.86	195.26	220.66
45/64	17.86	43.66	69.06	94.46	119.86	144.86	170.26	195.66	221.06
23/32	18.26	43.66	69.06	94.46	119.86	145.26	170.66	196.06	221.46
47/64	18.65	44.05	69.45	94.85	120.25	145.65	171.05	196.45	221.85
3/4	19.05	44.45	69.85	95.25	120.65	146.05	171.45	196.85	222.25
49/64	19.45	44.85	70.25	95.65	121.05	146.45	171.85	197.25	222.65
25/32	19.84	45.24	70.64	96.04	121.44	146.85	172.24	197.64	223.04
51/64	20.24	45.64	71.04	96.44	121.84	147.24	172.64	198.04	223.44
13/16	20.64	46.04	71.44	96.84	122.24	147.64	173.04	198.44	223.84
53/64	21.03	46.43	71.83	97.23	122.63	148.03	173.43	198.83	224.23
27/32	21.43	40.83	72.23	97.63	123.03	148.43	173.83	198.23	224.63
55/64	21.83	47.23	72.63	98.03	123.43	148.83	174.23	199.63	225.03
7/8	22.23	47.63	73.03	98.43	123.83	149.23	174.63	200.03	225.43
57/64	22.62	48.02	73.42	98.82	124.22	149.62	175.02	200.42	225.82
29/32	23.02	48.42	73.82	99.22	124.62	150.02	175.42	200.82	226.22
59/64	23.42	48.82	74.22	99.62	125.02	150.42	175.82	201.22	226.62
15/16	23.81	49.21	74.61	100.01	125.41	150.81	176.21	201.61	277.01
61/64	24.21	49.21	75.01	100.41	125.81	151.21	176.61	201.01	227.41
31/32	24.61	50.01	75.41	100.81	126.21	151.61	177.01	202.41	227.81
63/64	25.00	50.40	75.80	101.20	126.60	152.00	177.40	202.80	228.20

For example, 3 13/16in = 96.84mm.

INDEX